Jean,
Read this book! I hope it will help us both.
Happy (early) Birthday
Rita
June, 2007

W9-BSY-668

The Unofficial Guide For Living Successfully on Planet Earth

The Unofficial Guide For Living Successfully on Planet Earth

Barbra Gilman

Writers Club Press
San Jose New York Lincoln Shanghai

The Unofficial Guide For Living Successfully on Planet Earth

All Rights Reserved © 2001 by Barbra Gilman

Writers Club Press
an imprint of iUniverse.com, Inc.

For information address:
iUniverse.com, Inc.
5220 S 16th, Ste. 200
Lincoln, NE 68512
www.iuniverse.com

ISBN: 0-595-18023-X

Printed in the United States of America

DEDICATION

I dedicate this book to Lazaris, whose constant teachings have allowed me to reach my present state of consciousness and joy. He is a true beacon shining his love on all who wish to receive and experience conscious growth.

...and to Jamie, for filling me with the love and joy which served as the catalyst for the first half of this book seven years ago. His sense of humor, lightness of being and steady presence has taught me countless invaluable lessons.

...and to my daughter, Heather, who is the most precious gift I have ever been given. This book is to show her that miracles and magic really do exist, and to remind her that I love her like the sun, the moon, the stars and the t—s. And I always will! Her courage, creativity, and growth have been an inspiration to everyone!

...and to all those beings who know there is something more, something born of magic and miracles, and are willing to remember it! You never walk that path alone.

Finally, coming full circle, I dedicate this book to my mother, Frances, whose unconditional love has allowed me to be the woman that I am. This is my gift to her!

EPIGRAPH

Spirituality is the sacred center out of which all life comes, including Mondays and Tuesdays and rainy Saturday afternoons in all their mundane and glorious detail...The spiritual journey is the soul's life commingling with ordinary life.

~Christina Baldwin

CONTENTS

LIST OF EXERCISES

ACKNOWLEDGEMENTS

My ceaseless gratitude and love goes out to Lazaris, my teacher. If it were not for him, this book would never have been written. Throughout my twenty year journey toward remembrance of who I truly am and how all the pieces fit together, it has been Lazaris' information that has not only provided me with that knowledge but has shown me what to do with it. I am now combining Lazaris' lessons with everything else that I have uncovered on my life's journey, so that I may pass it on to you, the reader, praying that it will do as much for you as it has for me!

From a deep place within my heart, I want to express how blessed I have been for the gift of my soul group and family in this lifetime: Buddy who saw the wings I was given and let me fly free. I will always treasure his constant and gentle love; Tony, my spiritual sidekick, who has always been there encouraging and supporting my growth with his love and childlike exuberance; Harman, whose wisdom, friendship, generosity of spirit and healing energy has enriched my life. I am blessed by my soul sisters: Rona, Joan and Sylvia, who I love and cherish. What we have shared over the years could fill another book. In our friendships we have shared our joys, sorrows, laughter, growing pains and the kind of understanding that can only be found within the bond of sister souls.

Heartfelt thanks to my editor, Hal Zina Bennett, whose commitment and dedication to my vision has made this book possible. He has truly been an angel and a talented one at that!

Thanks to Heather Atlas for using her creative gifts to design a wonderful book cover, and…

To Jeff Young whose artistic talents brought that cover into creation.

Thanks also to my pre-publication readers: Dorothy Ann Jackson and Kathryn Kvols.

IN THE BEGINNING...

...there I was, working as a therapist for 20-plus years, when I realized that *most people do not need therapy!* Now clearly, this is not what you want to hear if you have just been through ten years of therapy. What I did find is that in order for people to create successful lives, which I believe is why most people go into therapy in the first place, they simply need an understanding of how they relate to the universe which, by the way, is what you will receive by reading this book. So all is not lost. But what do I mean when I say that people just want to understand how they relate to the universe? In the back of our minds, most of us have questions such as: Who am I? Why am I here? How do I relate to others? How do I create a successful life? Or, actually, how do I create *any life* for myself! These might seem like rather odd questions to ask, but these are the secrets that most of us have been missing.

You might be thinking, "Oh, come on, Barbra, how do I, little old me, create my life!" And I'll admit, the chances are pretty good that this was not a topic discussed at your dinner table when you were growing up. Which may help explain why the world is in such a mess. Well, thank God that life is different now! My greatest prayer is that these questions will now be the kinds of questions asked at dinner tables all over the world. Before we get there, we need to start at the beginning, which of course, is why I'm writing and you are reading this book.

When I was a small child I would sit at my window seat and speak to God. We were the best of friends. I would speak about how I wanted my life to be. We discussed all my dreams, never thinking that life would ever give me anything other than what I thought I wanted. For the first part of my life that was true, everything that I seemed to daydream (visualize) came true. At the time I had no idea about the power of desire and expectancy, having never heard of metaphysics.

In my twenties I married and soon gave birth to a beautiful baby girl. Strange things started happening, things that I definitely was not dreaming nor wishing for—or at least didn't think I was! These things lead up to a horrific divorce. I then set out—or should I say was forced out (by spirit)—to discover who I was. At the time it felt like everything I had believed in was crumbling at my feet, which by the way is how major change often begins in our lives. I always say that we become adults after we receive our first hurts. That is exactly what happened to me. What was worse, I was filled with negativity and fear, moving into a whole new world that I didn't believe I was equipped to handle. I was so horrified that God would allow this to happen to me that I gave up my relationship with Her! After three Hellish years, I discovered metaphysics. Or maybe I should say it came and found me. Not only did it save me, it changed my life in a way that nothing would ever be quite the same again!

I renewed my relationship with God/Goddess when I realized that I…not God/Goddess…had created my life to be as it was. Since then, my life has been about my own spiritual growth. Finding out what success means for me, and doing the work of creating that success, has sometimes left me retreating to my bed, laughing until I fell down on the floor, or crying out with joy! However, if you ask me if it was worth it, my answer is, "You bet your BMW it was!" There is nothing so fulfilling and thrilling than finding out who you are, taking back your power, and knowing you are doing something to change the world for the better. And by the way, everyone is here to change the world in his or her own way.

While on this adventure I noticed that in all people there is a series of programs (information) based on our original understandings of life, as learned when we were children. This information is, by the way, mostly false, and herein lies the problem: it all needs to be worked on.

When we start to work on these programs by changing, deleting, editing, etcetera, we end up with new programs, and these new programs are what start to create a new level of success in our lives. How do we do that? That is what this book is about!

When I use the word metaphysics in these pages, please don't be intimidated. I teach children and adults the same way. I believe in being simple, the way life really is, the way my brain works, without the very human impulse to complicate things. My goal in this book is to help you change your life, if that is what you desire. I'm giving you the simplest version of an incredibly complex field of information. I've added a good serving of fun to the mix. I've discovered in my workshops that this material really can be fun and this playful spirit opens us all up so that we can more easily take in this information.

I have been to many seminars and read many books. As I am taking in all the information and my brain is frying, I begin to realize that everything presented could have been said in one-quarter of the time! Of course, that's me: I like to learn in a way that is as quick and simple as possible. There are many people, I know, who don't feel they're getting their money's worth unless they chew endlessly on the issues. And, of course, some people just like to cram their heads with lots of information. Whichever of these categories you fit into, I do pray that this book will help you. Don't worry, your brain will still fry from all the information! So have no fear, you can always go out and get a book on quantum physics after you understand!

Are you ready? Great. Let's Begin! Where and how? Your constant companion as you read the pages ahead will be this book and a personal journal that will become your permanent record of the work you'll be doing here. There are some 38 exercises distributed throughout these pages. Do you really need to do them? The answer is yes, do them if you want to change your life. Do them if you want to experience success. Do them if you want to create a sense of fulfillment and joy in your life. (I know you heard that still small voice in your head, telling you to do them, to really get into these exercises. Come on now, don't deny it!)

You will discover that the exercises are like light switches. When you do them, the power comes on and you are showered with light. These exercises really do work—if you work! I recommend doing this work in a bound journal that you really like. There are plenty of beautiful bound journals available in bookstores. Choose one that feels good and looks good to you, one that you will enjoy carrying around with you to make notes or to study both while you are working with this book and afterwards.

If you haven't yet picked out a permanent journal for yourself, record the following on regular paper and transfer it to your journal when you get one.

✎ Exercise #1: The Victim Story

Choose an area of your life where you would like to create change. Using that area of your life as a reference point, think about a time when you felt like a victim. For example, if you would like to change something in your relationships, think about a situation involving relationships when you felt victimized or hurt. Write about how you felt. Go into explicit details about your feelings and thoughts, why you saw yourself as a victim and what part other people may have played in making you feel that way. Don't try to analyze these situations or make excuses why others did what they did, or why you did as you did. Just honor the feelings you are having and describe them as if that were the only truth in the world.

When you are done set your work aside for a moment. And now, move onto the next chapter.

1: MIRACLES, MAGIC AND JOY

We are living in the most exciting times on our planet Earth. For awhile I was believing that our mother (Earth) was in menopause. I can't remember if I read that somewhere or if it was because I'd been surrounded by friends who were experiencing this overwhelming, ever consuming dread of an apocalypse just around the corner. If I once halfway agreed with them, I must say that on closer inspection I have changed my belief. (By the way, it is actually good to change your beliefs every so often. I mean, come on now, wouldn't you feel rather silly if you were still waiting for the Easter Bunny each year! Surely you've changed that belief.) I now believe that our moody, excitable and ever-changing mother is actually in the process of giving birth! And it seems that her children are wrestling with all the jealousies and fears that older siblings usually exhibit as they anticipate a new family member coming into their lives.

Well, take heart dear siblings. We are not going to have to experience the 2 a.m. feedings or diaper changes that most of us would expect with younger siblings. This birth I'm speaking of announces a new paradigm shift in consciousness. This shift forces us to revise all the old maps of what life was about, how you live it, why you're here and how our lives are created. The changes we're talking about here are concepts that only a handful of people ever think about. But probably the only reason these ideas haven't been common knowledge is because there has never been anyone talking about them in ways that the rest of us could relate to!

The thoughts and ideas I'm talking about here are important not so much as abstractions for people to think about, however. Rather, it's important to learn what they are and to start living them in our daily lives.

1

If we can do that, they will make your dreams come true and make your reality the success that you want.

It is now time to bury the past with all the lies that we were brought into—such as, "father knows best" and the Cinderella mentality that our prince will show up with his golden carriage one day and make everything perfect. Clinging to these beliefs has only created the mediocrity and fear that we all live in now. Moreover, we have been so well programmed that we can't even see the lies any more. Not only did we accept them, we also educated ourselves in them, built our worlds around them, to the point of arrogance, defending them as the Truth. And now, to come face-to-face with the truth, is more than a little painful and scary. Admitting that we made a mistake or that we—God forbid!—might be wrong, is difficult. That old thing called ego gets in the way. I think you've heard of it!

Under the burden of those beliefs that we all too willingly accepted, we gave up our power, allowing ourselves to be controlled by authority figures we naively worshiped and believed in, only to find out that they make the Mafia look like beneficent angels. The blind leading the blind! It is now a time to awaken and be enlightened. Because of all these years of living at such an unconscious level we have created a wasteland of material addictions. We have lost touch with that which we really are. On the microcosmic level, we are functioning somewhere between late childhood and early adolescent levels. Having dysfunctional relationships, we haven't got a clue about how to create intimate relationships. What I am talking about has little if anything to do with sex, by the way. (We haven't a clue about that either!)

Did you ever stop to think that we are living in a civilization where the wives do not know who their husbands are, the husbands certainly don't have a clue to understanding who their wives are, the parents can't figure out their own kids, and the kids haven't got the foggiest idea what their own parents are about. About the only place any of us can experience unconditional love is with our cats or dogs! (Or birds or lizards or hamsters, etc.)

That condition of disconnection from everything and everyone who should matter to us doesn't just stop there, in our families. It extends out

to our relationships with the ⟨...⟩
allows us to ruin our air q⟨...⟩
everywhere, creating acid r⟨...⟩
causing the spread of AIDS⟨...⟩
inane international politic⟨...⟩
the weather, prejudice an⟨...⟩
judicial system, and an edu⟨...⟩
about violence on TV, and the⟨...⟩
to view the greatest art produce⟨...⟩

We are truly a mess and because of our ⟨...⟩ dear mother Earth pays the price. Meanwhile, we blithely con⟨...⟩ way, too busy being unconscious and not even caring, blinded by our own blatant arrogance! Now I realize, of course, that there are those people who are quite conscious of these issues. Some people even do something about them. We have Oprah, who is actually showing the way to consciousness on network television. However, please realize that this is still a minority. Most people are here for what I would say is a life of rest and relaxation: They work a nine-to-five job, come home, have a couple of beers or a piece of cheesecake (my choice), watch TV, go to sleep, start-up the next day and do it all over again. They are in a relationship that's not working. They have a job they don't like. And there they sit in their little mud puddle of discomfort, which seems like comfort because they've been there for so long. They do not know there is a way out, and if they could see it, their fear would probably stop them. They take their two weeks off in the summer and basically live by the belief that life is a struggle, you must pay taxes (another one of those false concepts), and then you die.

Now I realize that to anyone who is conscious enough to have picked up this book, all this sounds either incredibly sad or totally untrue. However, if you look around this world of ours, you'll quickly see that all of these things I describe really are going on—a little less here, a little more there. Now please don't get me wrong. I'm not a cynic nor do I walk on water. I'm just like everyone else, (because, after all, we really are all one!) moving

...ousness but still practicing and still learning! And I
... planet Earth things will probably never be perfect for
... developing our skills and learning our lessons.

...behavior that I just described is not an absolute that must
...hat way just because we are human beings. Not at all. Rather, it is
... of conditioning or programming, training that goes all the way
...to the womb. Since the world never gave out guide books about how to
...ate our reality (though they are available now!), most of us have simply
been waiting to see what life would serve up. Ours has been a trial and error
process, leading to a lot of errors. In other words, we simply kicked back and
accepted the defaults—i.e. the patterns others had already established—and
by doing so we simply fell into the mass programming which is mediocrity.
(Remember that it is much easier to control those that live in mediocrity as
opposed to those who live in freedom and possibility.) In order to heal the
problem we need to be able to look at it, recognize and take responsibility
for it, no matter how painful it might be. One of the problems that we all
face on this planet is that we have gotten really good at living in a constant
state of denial. (Some people seem to believe this is the 51st state,
protected by the Constitution.) It's true, of course, that it is actually much
more comfortable for us to run and hide under the bed than to
acknowledge what our lives have become. However, if you are reading this
book, you are one of those in the minority who are conscious and who are
looking to be even more so—and I applaud you!

Yes, this is such an exciting time to be alive. There is so much change
going on! In the next five to ten years we probably will not even recognize
our world! I believe that maybe we have done enough damage and so
reinforcements are being sent in, in the form of more God energy, angels,
guides, teachers and so forth. Or, maybe this was all in the plan! We won't
really know until we leave this lifetime. You will always find beliefs to
support people's theories, that's how it all works. (And if anyone ever tries
to tell you that their way is the only way, get out of there as fast as you
can!) I invite you to step out of your little mud puddle (we all have one)

and into the vast landscape that awaits you. Out in that bigger landscape you might just catch a glimpse of new possibilities for your life, possibilities that allow for miracles, magic and joy. If Turkey Hill could come up with Mint Oreo nonfat yogurt that tastes as good as Ben and Jerry's ice cream, anything is possible!

I like to remind people that even though this life we are leading is one of many, it is still the real thing and not merely a dress rehearsal. Here's a question: What would your life be like if you showed up as though it really mattered? What if there was no such thing as fear and you actually believed that whatever you set out to do you would accomplish! WOW! Think about it for a moment.

✎ Exercise #2: Commitment Statement

Write a statement of commitment to yourself. In it, try to describe exactly what you are willing to do to create the changes you want in your life. Be specific:

* How much time are you willing to spend each day, and at what time will that be?

* What will you have to give up in order to create the time? Are you willing to do this? How do you feel about that?

After writing the above, go on to write about how you will feel knowing that you have achieved the changed goals that you have set out for yourself. Write about your feelings and thoughts in a way that helps you get to know them very well, from the inside out. Think about whether or not you generally accomplish what you set out to do and explore in writing how do you feel about that. Remember, today is the first day of your new life!

✎ Exercise #3: Observations About Yourself

Write out three things you know and believe about yourself, your relationships in general, your relationships with your mother and your father, your role in that family, what you think and feel about money in general, what your relationship is to money, how you feel about your job or career, health in general, your state of health, your abilities, spirituality in general, your spirituality and your future. As you write about these things, don't forget to discuss what kind of impact each of these items have—how they help and support you, what they perhaps taught you, or how they have in some ways hindered you.

2: CHOOSING A PATH OF CHANGE

Okay, so you've gotten this far in the book. That means you have bought it, borrowed it, or manifested if from thin air. You've gotten through the first three exercises and you're ready to get to the good stuff that will change your life. Right? Wrong! Nothing out there is going to change your life. *You* are going to change your life, *only you!* And this moment is your point of power, the moment when you will take action. Remember, tomorrow never comes: it is always out there somewhere, just hanging around. If you want to know what you'll be like ten or twenty years from now, the answer is pretty simple: You will be exactly as you are today, only older, unless you choose to change now.

Change happens instantaneously. It begins the moment you have the intention to change. It's as if your higher self (we will get to that later) starts to work within your computer (your mind) to change all the old programming. It doesn't matter if only moments before your had decided on a no-change policy. If you have read this far, it's too late: You've already installed the new program which says "start change procedures now." You are already different. You now have the capabilities to proceed with that change.

This change takes work, I won't lie to you. It takes leaving your safe little mud puddle and venturing out on the most important exciting and scary adventure of your life. On this journey there will be times when you want to run and hide, or when you will break up in hysterical laughter. But isn't that what being here on Earth is all about?

Now, we could learn all our lessons on the high road, through love, joy, and fun. However, we human beings are not built that way. As long as we are here on this planet we have *stuff*. You know what I'm talking about. That stuff acts like a door, closing us off from the world, creating a barrier between you and what you desire. Think of a beautiful house on a magical tropical island, surrounded by magnificent foliage, wonderful aromas, the sounds of the ocean gently rolling on the shore, colors so beautiful that you can only imagine them in the dream world. Well, as long as your stuff is controlling your life you might as well be a prisoner inside that magnificent house, with the doors locked and heavy curtains drawn over all the windows. You would never be able to enjoy any of the beauty and joy of life. You might as well be living in a garbage dump because you have no access to any of it.

That is exactly what has happened to human beings. We have all our windows and doors shut. No one ever taught us there was another way, a way to open up to the magnificence of the world and who we really are; we are spiritual beings who are here having a physical experience so that we can remember and learn who we really are. We are here to discover the magic and miracles that we can create. All that we need is the intent and the willingness to grow, to open up all those windows and doors. We'll just start by opening a few locks. That's not too scary, right?

You would be amazed to discover what could happen just by having the clear intent to change. Remember, our dear mother Earth is a classroom where we do our work, learn our lessons and remember who we are. If we do not get it this time, we'll only have to come back and try it again. (But more on that later.) So, I say, why not get it this time around? You know, eat the broccoli now so you can get to the cheesecake.

✎ Exercise #4: Self-History

Write out a free flowing account of your life. Don't censor anything. Just write until there's no more to write. For some people that might be a page or two. For others it could be 30. When you're done, take a walk, take a shower or take a cookie break! Then come back and read your story. You might be amazed at what you'll find!

Now, edit your story and condense it down to a single theme, only one paragraph long. Then narrow this down to one sentence and then to one powerful word. If the word has negative connotations, such as fear or humiliation, change it to whatever its 180 degree opposite would be for you. Now take that positive word, and create a sentence from it, then a paragraph and then a free flowing story, which will serve as the map for your journey.

And what is all this about? It is about becoming conscious. How do you choose to become conscious? Well, if you've gotten this far in the book, part of you, your higher self, already knows how and is guiding you in this direction. It's just a question of getting all your different parts to go along with the program. You know, there is that little child hiding in the corner, stamping her/his feet saying, "No! Please don't take me there." What you should know is that the easiest way to become more conscious is just to have clear intention and willingness.

Many people say they want spiritual enlightenment, or want to raise their consciousness. We have all heard the New Age buzzwords, or maybe have even read some books or attended some classes. However I can tell you that there is a big difference between reading all the right books and taking all the right seminars and being able to *talk the talk*. It is quite another thing to *walk the talk*, that is, to live the information every day. That's where the work really comes in. Let's admit it, that little child within us simply does not like hard work. It's like the old story of going to church every Sunday and coming home to attack your husband with the vacuum cleaner. It's very easy to declare yourself a New Age person; it's quite another to live it.

✎ Exercise #5: Discovering Awareness

This four part exercise is designed to expand your ability to become more conscious of your awareness, how to focus your awareness, and how to actually stretch it. Think of this exercise as being a little like playing with a piece of dough, kneading it, stretching it, discovering you can mold it in different ways. The more you practice this awareness, the more you will gain the ability to de-stress your life. Keep in mind that the benefits of this exercise come with practice; just as with learning to swim or ride a bike or play tennis, your abilities expand in direct proportion to how much you practice.

One: Choose an object in the room where you are sitting. Focus your eyes on it, and then bring your full awareness to it for one full minute. During that time period if your mind wanders simply bring it back to focus on your object.

Two: Choose two more objects in the room, so that you now have three objects that you will be focusing on. This time, divide your awareness between these three objects, giving one of them your full attention, then switching to another, then to the third. As your attention expands, add objects until you have five on which you can hold your awareness, switching from one to another.

Three: Now do the exact same exercise as above, with all five objects, only this time, tell yourself to relax and reduce the effort that you're using to divide your awareness between the five objects.

Four: Now, instead of focusing just on objects, choose a memory or a mental image and bring your full awareness to it for one minute.

Five: Close your eyes. In a similar way that you did with the objects, now focus and then divide your awareness between three memories or mental images.

Six: Now do the exact same exercise as above (with all three mental images or memories) but this time tell yourself to reduce the effort that you're using.

Seven: In your journal, write about what you have experienced in the above exercise. Particularly pay attention to how it helped you realize how much ability you actually have to choose where you put your attention.

In the twenty-plus years that I have been consciously following a spiritual path, I have met many people at all levels of growth. They all have stuff. Some have persuasive sales pitches, almost convincing you that they've got it. Some really mean it but don't live it and wonder why it doesn't work for them. Only a handful actually live it every day, and you know what? They still have their stuff. It soon becomes very clear that having stuff is just part of being human, and this is the thing to understand here: we all have humanity and divinity.

To understand this concept, think of some famous people that you know of, the ones who appeared to have everything in the world going for them. All of a sudden you read in the newspapers that they got caught with drugs or prostitutes or they slammed into some wall at 100 miles an hour in their new Porsche. What's going on here is that their divinity, that aspect of themselves that is open to God energy, which just flows through allowing them to do what they do so well, to use the gift that they are here in this lifetime to share, is doing great. However, they haven't taken a good look at their own humanity. People who have such an incredible divinity side sometimes forget that there is that humanity side, too. It's easy to overlook when everything else in your life seems to be going so well. It is the combination of our humanity and our divinity that gives us our balance and wholeness.

What do we do when our stuff shows up on our doorstep? One thing for sure, we don't slam the door in its face. That's usually our first instinct. The second one is to run and hide under the bed. There is only one way to free yourself from the burden of your stuff, and that is to bless it because—guess what, it brings a gift with it, and it's not just a set of plastic Tupperware! You can do a dance with it (the conscious slide) and in no time it is gone, leaving you on a higher level of consciousness. Joseph Campbell once said, "Where you stumble, there your treasure is!" And he was right. Welcome in your stuff and your gift will be revealed to you.

✎ Exercise #6: Divinity And Humanity

This is a valuable journaling exercise that focuses your attention on how our lives reflect our divinity and humanity. There are two questions to ask yourself, then a letter to write:

a. Where do you think your divinity shows up in this lifetime? How do you experience it? How do you express it?

b. What part(s) of your humanity do you feel needs work?

c. Write a letter to that part of your humanity that needs work. Explain that you realize it is your lesson in this lifetime to do this work, and that it comes with a gift for you. Tell your humanity that you're ready and willing to learn the lesson, and ask for its help, then thank it and bless it and release it.

I must caution you, it takes a while to get to a welcoming place with your gift. Most of us must travel through the valley of the shadow of doubt and walk through the fire of fear before we are bathed in the clear, fresh waters of joy, and cradled in the arms of trust. Is it worth the struggle? You bet your Beemer it is!

There are more and more people the world over who are opening their eyes from that deadly sleep of unconsciousness. This is the only way to save our planet. What a miracle, our species finally evolving. (Won't it be great to be walking on two legs at last?) Thirty years ago you couldn't speak about this stuff to just anyone without having the little men with the white coats coming to cart you away. If you went to a human potential seminar (if you could find one) there would be twenty people in the room, at most. If you wanted to buy a book on the subject you'd have to go to a metaphysical book store on some back street in one of the big cities, like New York or Chicago or San Francisco or Los Angeles. Now it is mainstream: God, angels, and communicating with those in the spirit world are front page news. Oprah is teaching meditation on TV. Alternative medicine is growing by leaps and bounds, and a few insurance companies are actually paying for these methodologies. Metaphysical TV shows and movies are showing up everywhere, even sitcoms throw around the jargon. Any day the President will be telling us that they have made U.F.O. contact. (Less than a decade off, some say.) What a world!

Please understand, nothing I am speaking of is new. We are talking here about timeless wisdom. We are simply becoming more aware of it. The cover-up is over. And as more people become aware of this information we reach critical mass, which simply means that the momentum of these believers is such that it automatically brings a new level of awareness to the whole population of the world.

There is an incredible study called the "100th Monkey Syndrome." In 1979, biologist Lyall Watson published his book *Lifetide,* the story of a monkey tribe on an island near Japan. A vast amount of freshly dug sweet potatoes covered with sand were dumped on this island. Up until then, the monkeys' traditional food required no preparation and they were not too excited about eating the dirty potatoes. However, one bright monkey solved the problem by taking the potatoes down to the water and washing them off. One by one the other monkeys started to do the same. The incredible part is that at a certain point in time, when about 100 monkeys had acquired this knowledge, other monkeys on other islands, having no physical contact with the original monkeys, started washing their potatoes also!

Are we as intelligent as the monkeys? One would hope.

In a time of transition, such as the one our planet is going through now, one really needs to be laser-focused and committed to learning as much as they can about themselves and about becoming more conscious. I know that's scary. But one of the things we have to learn is that we've got nearly everything backwards. Most of what we've been told in our lives is a lie, or at least an "untruth." What is the motive for doing that? To keep us controlled. Remember, fear based people are easy to control. Just keep the road to personal power out of their reach or make it look absolutely foolish, and they will soon be feeling frustrated and impotent. Remember the Woody Allen movie, *Sleeper,* when Woody wakes up in the future and finds out that eating steak and smoking cigarettes is really good for you? After reading this book, something like that just might happen to you, and you'll have a great breakthrough, realizing you need not be limited by your stuff and your early learnings.

The world is in transition because somewhere on our journey we made a wrong turn, probably at the junction of spiritual growth drive and money, power and Greed Street. We gave up our power, succumbed to fear and the so-called "good life." We fell into a coma and woke up when we found out that some food chemists somewhere had invented fat-free food. We suddenly realized that our Earth was not in the best shape anymore. Most of us had become empty shells trying to own two homes and a couple of Mercedes. The antidote is to commit to having clear intention, to be willing and ready to create your fullest potential, and to become an enlightened spiritual being. At that point your higher self rolls up her/his sleeves and the adventure begins.

On to the next chapter, but only after doing exercise seven!

✎ Exercise #7: Rating Your Commitment Level

a. On a scale from 1 to 10, how much stuff do you allow to be thrown into your life to keep you off track, so that your fullest potential remains unknown to you? (A rating of 10 means you do it a lot.)

b. What kind of stuff do you let impede you in this way?

c. On the same scale of 1 to 10 rate yourself, on the level of commitment that you have, in the journey of fulfilling your greatest potential. (Consider 10 to be the highest level of commitment.)

d. Create a new level of commitment for your self. For example, if your present commitment level is 6, move it up to 10 and ask yourself what you will do to maintain that level of commitment. What will you cease to put in your own way?

3: God, Goddess, All That Is…Is All There Is!

We start our journey here because there is nothing that is not part of God/Goddess All That Is. I am not going to go into a long dissertation about what God is. For those who are interested in doing that I would recommend Neale Donald Walsch's *Conversations with God,* one of my all-time favorite books. But just to make sure we are traveling on the same path together, I offer the following:

When most of us think of God, it is almost impossible not to think of an incredibly large man with a long white beard sitting on a throne in heaven. This image has been fostered by the movies as well as some of the pictures that remain for us from our childhoods. Clearly, it's a image that needs to be updated not only in our brains but, more importantly, in our hearts. We need to have a deeper knowledge of God's presence and to realize that it is a divine force that resides within each one of us. It is only in this manner that we will be able to find the trust and peace we so desperately seek. And when we finally accept that concept we will realize we had the trust and peace we have been seeking all along!

God is an energy, and as with all energy it is composed of both the masculine and the feminine, which is why you will see me write it as God/Goddess, with "All That Is" always inferred. Keep in mind that there is nothing in the universe that is not composed of the energy that is God/Goddess. And this energy is omnipotent, omnipresent, and omniscient—the most powerful energy there is!

Each of us only perceives God/Goddess from the perspective of our own consciousness. There are some, for example, who see their God as a punishing God, one who dictates the philosophy of an eye for an eye, and a tooth for a tooth, a vengeful and judgmental God. I think most of us would like to believe that such concepts are part of the past. But I'm afraid that's not the case. As bizarre as it might seem, there are plenty of people in the world today who still perceive their God in this way.

I guess that tells us how far we've come! And just maybe, it is with this concept of God that all our problems begin!

One of the problems we must come to terms with is that we have always allowed other people to tell us who God is rather than experiencing God for ourselves. We have assigned one day of the week when we publicly acknowledge God, by "going to the place where God dwells"— i.e. church, synagogue, mosque—and when we get there we have someone stand up in the front of the room and explain to us who God/Goddess is. But let me remind you, the God they describe to you is always through their own perception.

You are a spiritual being who is here on Earth experiencing physical existence, and an important part of that experience involves keeping your relationship with God/goddess alive and ever-growing. This can only happen if you are willing to trust and explore your own experience.

Now and then I hear people wondering aloud, "What would God/Goddess think of my actions now?" What always comes to my mind is that this is a real "God-fearing person," and I simply have to shake my head in disbelief! I wish they could really hear what they're saying. The question I would pose to them is this: "What if you were the parent of a one-year old girl just starting to walk, and as the she was exploring her environment she tips over the a flower vase, water and all? What would your reaction be? Would you punish this child, maybe beat her? Would you condemn her to three days of bread and water? If you answered anything other than "clearly not," please get some help!

Do you believe that God/Goddess would be any less forgiving and supportive with you or me as we explore our environment, our lives here on Earth? Of course not. No matter what you might have been taught,

God/Goddess is not judgmental, vengeful or punishing; rather, God/Goddess is pure unconditional love. And just as the most loving parent would do for her own child, you are given everything, in the form of free will. A loving parent only wants to see you happy, healthy and enjoying abundance. God/Goddess will never step in and interfere with your free will—not even when you yourself are judging yourself. God/Goddess knows that your actions and even your judgments are merely illusions and no real harm can come to you. You have been given everything you need for a successful and happy life. You only need to have the willingness to receive, and the knowledge of how all this will work for you. It is in this knowledge that most of us fall a little short, and it is here that we shall begin.~

✎ Exercise #8: God/Goddess

Draw a vertical line (lengthwise) down the center of a piece of paper or a page in your journal so that you have two equal sized columns.

In the left column write out all your beliefs in God, including those from your childhood.

In the right column write out the beliefs from the left side that you would choose to best describe the God/Goddess you want to believe in now. Add any new beliefs you feel would better serve you.

Now be those positive beliefs in your everyday life by asking yourself what God/Goddess would do in each situation which arises.

Pray.

4: It's All About Energy

I am now going to offer you the most awesome idea that you are likely to hear in your whole life: *You create your own reality.* Maybe you should just sit still for a few minutes and contemplate what that might actually mean if it really were true—which it is. How would it affect your life? What might you do differently if you were living every moment guided by this concept? And for those of you who already believe you know all this, keep reading anyway. At least for a while. Maybe, just maybe, you will discover something new along the way. It could be that you haven't fully grasped how this concept can impact your life. If you had you probably wouldn't have been led to this book. (Remember, the greatest obstacle to learning is often what we believe we already know.)

Now, of course, the question is this: *How do we each create our own realities?* And maybe even, *If this is so, why in the world did I create this one?* The first part of the answer is that you created it with your energy, energy that is in turn created by your thoughts and feelings, that is, with the perceptions and feelings that make you who you are. Think of this energy as going out into the universe like little magnets and bringing back to you the physical manifestations of these thoughts and feelings. For example, if you believe this book will change your life it will, and if you don't you can rest assured that it won't.

As simple as it is, this is one of the most important concepts you can ever get. Keep in mind, though, that simple ideas have a tendency to be overlooked, under-looked and not seen at all! We humans, after all, like to make things complicated.

The trick here is to understand this information, then bring it down from your brain to your heart where you can own it, live it, and where it will become your wisdom. As long as it is only in your brain, as an intellectual idea, it won't mean too much, other than to provide you with a great concept to throw around at cocktail parties.

Very simply put, this is how we create our realities. You have your own energy frequency, which is produced by everything that goes on in your life. That energy reaches out into the world around you, drawing back to you whatever matches your frequency. It is through the energy of your thoughts and feelings that you can change your life. Now, you might be saying, *Hmm!* or even, *So?* Well, if there was just one thing you need to get in this lifetime, this is it! And if you can truly get it you will be empowered and set free! Because you will know that no one but you can be responsible for your life. And if you are not happy or fulfilled, you will know who you can turn to for changing it!

✎ Exercise #9: Change Your Mind, Change Your Life

a. Go back to exercise #4 and read again what you wrote about your life.

b. Looking at what you've created so far in your life, make a list of the things you like about it. Make a list of what you dislike.

c. What ongoing thoughts and feelings that you presently hold are responsible for creating these things? (Think about thoughts and feelings that help to create both the things you like about your life and the things you dislike.)

Albert Einstein stated that everything in the universe is composed of energy. Everything! That's right, everything in the universe!

Now, when I speak of energy I am talking about God, the energy that God is, and that means everything. Moreover, that energy cannot be destroyed or diminished; it simply changes form or is recycled, which is true whether we are talking about grains of sand on the beach or our own reincarnation. You, your dog, your car, the trees, the sidewalk, everything that you see and everything you do not see (that's the fun part) is composed of energy. This energy can take the form of actual substances that we shape to create our reality. The only difference between energy which is invisible and just floating around in the universe and the energy that comprises the chair you're sitting in is the frequency of their vibrations.

✎ Exercise #10: Experiencing Energy

Place your hands together, palms touching, and rub them together vigorously, as you would if you were trying to warm them up. Now, stop rubbing and just hold your hands palm to palm for a moment. Very slowly start to draw your palms apart a few inches, cupping them slightly. Focus your awareness on the feelings in your hands. After a moment, you will begin to feel the energy generated in the space between them. Now slowly move your hands further apart and be aware of the feeling of the energy. Then continue moving them back and forth and you will feel the changes in the energy. This energy is who you are, and it is the same energy that God is.

If you need healing energy, simply ask God/Goddess to make you an open channel for healing energy. Then visualize white light coming down from the universe, through the top of your head and out through your cupped hands. Place your hands anywhere that you feel any discomfort. Or simply use the same technique to energize your body. Then you can throw away your Tylenol bottle!

Close this exercise by writing about your experience in your journal.

For a moment, think of a TV or radio. When you tune in a station and get a particular program, what do you have? What you have are different bands of frequency, each channel holding different sets of vibrations. You receive the frequency or channel that you want by tuning into it. Obviously, you are not getting a real person sitting inside your TV or radio but their energy is moving across the airwaves into your home. In a very real way, who we are—our thoughts and feelings—creates our reality in much the same way that we tune in stations or channels on a radio or TV.

Our lives are simply the interplay of different energy exchanges, the denser energies (anger and fear) having a lower rate of vibration while the lighter frequencies (love and joy) have a higher rate of vibration.

Here's a little picture to play with in your imagination. Imagine a skyscraper that has 100 floors. The basement is where the lower frequencies or denser energies exist. (Here's a little clue, I use the words "frequency" and "consciousness" interchangeably.) Now, I am sure that you must know at least one person whose consciousness fits down there. I certainly know some who do! As we go up the skyscraper, we keep increasing frequencies at each level, all the way up to the penthouse (100th floor) where we have the highest frequencies, which is God consciousness. (Most of us will no longer be in our physical bodies when we reach that level!) One of the reasons we're here, is to keep raising our level of consciousness until we reach that level of God consciousness.

For a moment, assume that you are here on Earth to experience these different frequencies of energy. Each person who enters your life, and any situations you create, are simply frequencies of energy that we are tuning into and learning from. Our ability to experience one or the other is based on where we are at any given point in our own frequency or consciousness. Each frequency we tune into teaches us some lesson, and each lesson comes with a gift. Of course, wouldn't you know that we do not get the gift until we learn the lesson!

Each vibration within a frequency has a color and a number, like the floors in our skyscraper. Each level is painted a different color, with each person having a specific vibration field (a pattern of shape and color) around them, called an aura. That's like when you see the glow around a candle flame. Now, your aura has a color field which is constantly changing as your mental, emotional or spiritual states change. For example, its shape and color will be one way when you are joyful, another when you are sad. At the same time, your aura develops a certain pattern, always a certain color and number which is your frequency, determined by who you are. And you will always manifest that same color/number frequency in the form of a person or situation (physical manifestation) in the outside world. What you manifest will be a mirror image of who you are at that time.

Can you imagine! It's a good thing that most people can't see auras, since we already have a difficult time accepting the few shades of people that we have on this planet. What would we do if we could see every color of the spectrum running around? Here's one answer: When we raise our frequency (consciousness) we automatically tune into the frequency of love, loving everyone!

I said that when you have learned your lesson you get the gift, and I am sure you want to know what that gift is going to be. The gift is raising your frequency, that is, raising your consciousness, which changes your color/number, thus allowing you to bring in another lesson that is now on a higher level, sort of like creating better and better things for your life. It's like moving from the damp and dusky basement to the penthouse! And when you learn all your lessons you can graduate. But more about that later. If you do not learn the lessons at any frequency level you are working on, you will come back to work on the same lesson again. It's sort of like going to summer school.

Let me offer an example: Amy is a client of mine, and one of the things she wanted to work on was creating a healthy working relationship. I asked her to tell me what her ideal relationship would look like. This is what she said: "I would like to create a man who was my friend, someone who is in touch with his feminine energy, totally vulnerable in the emotional department, very nurturing, very spiritual, really generous and someone who loves to have fun."

"Wow!" I said, "you and every other woman. You just created Mr. Right! That's the guy who lives on the 90th floor of our skyscraper."

I asked Amy to tell me something about herself in relation to those aspects she wanted in him. I asked, "How are you as far as being vulnerable with your own emotions?"

"Well," she replied, "because I was brought up in a dysfunctional family, it's hard for me to be open with my emotions, even though I do try."

"Okay," I said, "what about nurturing? How are you in this area?"

"Well," she said, "I guess it's really the same as my first answer. One doesn't learn how to be nurturing when you come from a dysfunctional family, you know."

Moving right along, I asked about her level of spirituality.

Her answer was that she was so busy trying to get ahead in her career that she had absolutely no extra time to do any meditation or reading or any sort of spiritual work.

"Well, what about your generosity level?"

Again came an answer about her dysfunctional family and how there were so many people grabbing at her food and clothes that it was hard for her to be generous.

Finally we got to the last question. "What about fun in your life?"

She shook her head.

"So, what you're saying, Amy, is that you live on the 5th floor of our skyscraper."

Then I asked Amy, "If you are living on the fifth floor of our skyscraper and you happen to be out in the corridor walking around, would it be possible to bump into someone who is living on the 90th floor?"

Amy shook her head slowly and sadly.

"I rest my case," I said. "But let's not stop here. Let's ask another question, and this is the really important one. What would a person living on the 5th floor have to do to meet that guy on the 90th floor?"

Amy thought for a moment, then answered, "I guess they would have to get in the elevator and go up to that floor."

I nodded emphatically. "Right!" And that's exactly what Amy had to do in her life. She had to raise her frequency, her consciousness. Because all the men she was drawing into her life from her present frequency were at the same level of consciousness as her. They were all fifth floor guys. If she wanted to meet Mr. Right, she was going to have to work on herself, raising her vibration or consciousness. She had to get herself onto the 90th floor before she started creating the reality she was seeking.

You see it's actually quite simple: You get who you are!

Here's another example: We have two people walking south on the street—Bob and Tim. Bob is what you would call a very positive person. He thinks life is great and expects wonderful things to happen to him. He walks briskly, with his head up, clothes always immaculate and he always has a beautiful smile. So let's say that Bob is vibrating at a frequency of 40 and his aura is a very pretty shade of blue.

On the other hand we have Tim. He thinks he's a screw up and is convinced that everything that happens to him sucks. He walks with his head down, his clothes are always messy, and his mouth is fixed in a perpetual frown. You know the type. Let's say that he is vibrating at a frequency of 10 and his aura is the color brown.

Now walking in the other direction going north we have Fred. He is operating at a frequency of 7, also the color brown. Fred is out to rob someone! Who do you think will be his victim, Bob or Tim? He robs Tim. Tim, after all, has the frequency/color of a victim and so attracts this energy to him. When thinking about this example, however, keep one thing clear: the person who committed the crime is still responsible for his actions. Tim may be putting out the signals that he is an easier mark than Bob but he does not compel Fred to rob him. The message here is not to blame the victim but to recognize that we can make new choices to attract the very best energy to us.

✎ Exercise #11: Looking at Your Energy Level

a. Looking back at what you have just read, ask yourself at which floor of our skyscraper metaphor that you normally function.

b. Now look at your closest relationships and write down at what floors they normally function.

c. Now write about the lessons that each of these people has brought, or continues to bring into your life, and what will it take for you to complete each of these lessons?

d. Looking into your past relationships, especially those that might have been particularly difficult or painful, see if you can find what lessons they were bringing to you. Did you learn these lessons? If so, where did the gift bring you?

e. What floor of our skyscraper would you like to be functioning at? And what will you need to do to get there?

Here's another little tidbit about energy. You know how sometimes when you're with another person in a relationship, there is always something you want to change about them? It doesn't matter if it's your spouse, a close friend, or a co-worker. Never go into a relationship trying to change someone, because that's just setting yourself up for failure.

Needless to say we still have those people in our lives that we'd like to change. But the bottom line is that you can't change this other person; however, what you can do is change your self. Here lies another universal principal, when you have two frequencies vibrating at the same level, if you change one frequency the other one has to change. That's universal law. Now that doesn't necessarily mean that it will change in the direction that you want it to, it simply means that it will change in some way!

Here's another example for you to mull over: Marilyn was a client of mine, her husband was an executive and he was always either busy at work or busy on the golf course, which left absolutely no time for them to spend together.

When Marilyn first heard this concept of change, she decided that she would change herself. She based this on the principle that her husband would have to change, so she started her plan.

Marilyn decided that for the next month or so whenever her husband came to tell her that he was off to the golf course, she would tell him that this was fine with her because she was also busy doing things that were fun for her. By the way, this was not true. She was only making it up.

After this went on for awhile, Marilyn told me what she had been doing and asked why it wasn't working. The answer was easy. Because Marilyn was only making up these adventures her frequency did not actually change. Obviously, nothing had changed in her frequency so there was nothing to create change in her husband's. Now that Marilyn understood that she actually had to change, we created a program to allow her to do just that.

I asked Marilyn what would she be doing if her husband was there to spend time with and she had a whole list of things they would do: go on picnics, visit friends, go to the museum, etc. So I told her that she needed to actually do these things, to make believe that he wasn't even in her life. She should do the things that would make her happy!

In a short time Marilyn reported that she actually was having fun in her life and she wondered why she hadn't done these things by herself long before. She actually stopped thinking about trying to create ways to have her husband join her.

Then one weekend her husband came to her and asked if she would like to spend the weekend together. Very calmly she reported back to him that she would love to but she already had plans and asked if she could have a rain check for the next weekend!

Marilyn now found out that the universal principal holds true-change one frequency and the other one has to move somewhere, and in this case her husband moved right into the frequency she had in mind! As an extra bonus Marilyn discovered a little bit more about herself and expanded her life!

Here's another thought about trying not to change someone else. When you have someone in your life whose behavior, to you, is like hearing the sound of fingernails scratching on a blackboard, here's what you can do. Because you continually think of the negative behavior of that person you are literally holding their frequency (and their behavior) in place by your energy. You are thinking, "That's the way they are!" And guess what? You are right. That is the way they are as long as you hold them that way!

What you need to do is think about them the way you want them to be. Your feelings will go along with your new perception. In doing so, you are creating a space for them to change and the energy to help them.

When my daughter was a teenager, she went through a stage where she simply did not want to have a mom that was different from all the other moms. Who me? Yes, clearly, the mom I was, well, maybe a little different than the others. I was a "metaphysical mom," who didn't yell, who tried to teach about consciousness and spirituality, and who wanted to be a friend as well as a mom to my daughter. Well, that was simply too strange. I had doors slammed in my face any time I would use words that sounded "weird" to my daughter!

At the time I felt like such a victim. It just didn't make sense to me. I used to tell my daughter, "If I had a mom like me I'd be flying through the sky right now!"

But all my efforts were to no avail. My arguments fell on deaf ears! I found myself telling my victim story to my girlfriends, getting answers like, "Well, that's just kids, isn't it?"

One day I was speaking to a client who had a child who was treating her in a similar way. I heard myself giving her the same advice I should have been giving myself: "The solution is easy. Just don't keep holding that resonance on them!"

Wow! It hit me the moment I said it. There it was, the answer to my victim story. As they say, we teach best what we most need to learn! Being the good student that I am, I listened to my own words. Within the month my daughter's behavior began changing. I was still known as the weird mom, but I was able to sleep at night.

✎ Exercise #12: Changing You First

a. Where in your life are you trying to change someone else?

b. What can you do to change your perspective of the situation?

c. What can you do to change you?
d. Bring the person into your meditation and communicate with them there.
e. Send your higher self to their higher self, to help work it out.
f. Surround them in white light and release them for the highest good of all.

Here are the ingredients of success: If you were setting out to create an award-winning cheesecake, you would need to have specific high quality ingredients. The chances are pretty good that if you scrimp a little here and a little there, what you get is going to be a scrimped cheesecake, not an award-winning one.

Creating your reality also calls for specific high quality ingredients, and the good news is, it won't be as fattening as your cheesecake! The ingredients you'll need are as follows: imagination, desire, and expectancy.

Imagination: You have used the skill of imagination since childhood. Actually, that's probably where it had the most use. But you know what they say, "It's never too late." So start practicing. Start out by visualizing. You know, that is daydreaming with a purpose. You simply create thoughts and images and feelings of what you want to have in your life. Close your eyes and watch your thoughts become a movie on the lids of your closed eyes. For increased value, create color, and sound. Like anything else, it will get easier with practice. You may find that you don't get anything at first. But it's like learning anything new. The rewards are few at first, but with tenacity and patience you will soon be an expert.

Desire: If you look back at your life and remember something that you wanted and did create, you'll see that you had a lot of desire or passion about it. You can say that desire is an incredibly strong feeling (strong vibrations) and that is exactly what you need if you are to create what you want. Your desire actually pulls what you want right to you, giving increased energy to your *magnets.*

Expectancy: After you do the work of deciding what it is that you want, creating beliefs that will be in alignment with what you desire, using your imagination in the form of visualizations, holding the resonance (see below) of what it is that you want to create, it is now time to act as if you already have it! This is expectancy.

Here's a good example: Jennifer wanted a dog. However, at the time she couldn't afford the prices that the local breeders were asking. So she called the animal shelter and gave a rough description of what she was looking for, a shaggy little dog, preferably a puppy, with an affectionate disposition. The woman at the shelter told her to come down because they had many animals to choose from and she thought that Jennifer might be able to find what she was looking for.

When Jennifer arrived she immediately spotted the exact puppy she had visualized. But it was walking out of the shelter with another young woman, whose face was just beaming with joy. Poor Jennifer! She went inside and simply could not find a dog that she felt any attachment to, especially after seeing that little shaggy puppy of her dreams walking out in the arms of the other woman.

When Jennifer returned home, a friend called and asked what had happened at the shelter. When Jennifer told her friend the story, the friend reminded her of the missing ingredient—expectancy—and asked Jennifer why she didn't bring a leash and collar with her? Bringing these items along was both a clear signal and confirmation that she was prepared and that she completely trusted she was going to get a dog that day. That was it, Jennifer realized. She was missing the one ingredient that would have allowed her to walk out with the shaggy puppy.

That week Jennifer went out and shopped for everything that she would need for her little puppy—a bed, toys, food and a leash and collar. Once again she made the trip to the shelter. However this time she was the one walking out with the puppy and a face beaming with joy!

✎ Exercise #13: Rounding Up the Ingredients

a. Make a list of the areas of your life that you want to work with. For each specific area:

b. Write about what your desire is—what it is you really want to have, what you want to change or achieve.

c. Use your imagination and create a visualization, which you will run, like a miniseries in your head, of how your life will be when you have finally brought into it all that you desire.

d. Coming from expectancy, what do you need to do, for each of your desires, to prepare a space for their fulfillment in your life?

Here are two little tricks for successfully manifesting:

Anchors (NLP): Did you ever hear a song and instantaneously travel back through time to some wonderful experience such as your first love? Or, can you remember what it feels like when you're looking through your rear view mirror and you see a flashing red light 10 feet behind you! These are anchors. An anchor can be a word, a touch, a sound or an object. It can be something we feel, see, hear, taste or smell. Anchors have the incredible power to instantaneously create emotions and sensations.

Remember Pavlov's dogs salivating when they heard a bell ringing, announcing that food was coming? That's how anchors work with us humans. They set up strong expectations within our entire being.

Anchors are everywhere especially in the world of advertising. Even my dog gets hungry when she sees the golden arches, and she's a vegetarian! When you are in an intense emotional state and a specific stimulus is provided at the peak of that state, the stimulus and emotional state become neurologically linked. Then, whenever the stimulus is once again triggered, the intense emotional state will automatically occur. Putting it simply, it's the way we're wired!

Now let's learn how to create this magic: The first thing you do is think of an emotion that you would like to be able to access any time you want, such as love, joy, courage, confidence, etc. Okay, you can do sexiness! That's close enough.

The next thing is to think of a past experience where you felt this emotion. It can be any time in your past, whether you were two years old or twenty or just yesterday. What is important here is simply that you are feeling the experience. Now close your eyes and actually bring yourself back into that experience. See what you were seeing then, hear what you were hearing then, and feel the emotions you were feeling.

Now, build up the feelings of that time until you reach a peak where it feels so good that you think you are going to explode! At this point, take any two fingers and gently push them together for the count of four. At that moment open your eyes and your fingers at the same time.

You have just created an anchor. Congratulations! Now you simply repeat that process about ten times. This is called "stacking anchors." To test your anchor, simply take the same two fingers and push them together. At that moment the feeling should fill your whole body! Do this stacking of 10 a few times a day.

Remember, with any exercise like this practice moves you from effort to expert. It's sort of like going to the gym and doing a set of repetitions ten times each in order to build your muscles. The only difference is that here you are building your life!

Now, whenever you want to experience the feelings you have anchored, all you need to do is push your fingers together and voila! Here's the thing: whenever you create an anchor, remember to write down which fingers represent which anchor (i.e. right thumb and index finger = joy). Don't mix up your anchors…like going for forgiveness and pushing your sexy anchor! Or, maybe that would work!

✎ Exercise #14: Anchors Away!

Think about areas of your life that you would like to work on. Decide on which emotion(s) you would like to use as an anchor. You might find that you would like more than one emotion for your anchor; that's fine, simply follow the same procedure I've described (in the text) for each emotion but just remember to keep them all on the same anchor. I call this a "recipe anchor"—containing a little of this and a little of that.

Area of your life	Emotion(s) in anchor	Placement

Now Stack Away!

Holding the resonance: When you want to create something in your life, think, feel and act as if you already have it. And add your anchor!

Here's an example: Scott was a wonderful teenaged boy that I was working with. He absorbed everything that he learned like a sponge, just as most young people do. Scott wanted a car. His father told him they couldn't afford it right now, so he came to me for advice. I told Scott to create the knowingness of having the car already. Then I told him, that while he was in his room looking outside, he should think to himself, "Gee, my car is parked in the garage and Dad will be home soon. I better move it so Dad can park there!" Then he would imagine doing just that. Also, I suggested that he might think thoughts such as, "Boy, I should go out there and wash my car so it will really look great!"

Being the believer that Scott was, he followed these directions to the tee. He said he had lots of fun doing it! Two weeks later, Scott's dad came home, told Scott that he had just ordered a new car and that Scott could have the old one! ~

✎ Exercise #15: Holding the Resonance

Write down the story line of what it is you will be holding a resonance on. Be very specific in describing all the senses—what will it look like, what will it feel like, what will it sound like? Create a time period—specific holidays are always good. You can add a Christmas tree, religious image, Easter Bunny, a birthday cake, or whatever to your picture to specify your time period. And don't forget to specify the year. You don't want to wait ten years to get all of this working in your life!

5: Change Is Wonderful

As soon as people begin to understand that they create their own reality based on their thoughts and feelings, they start to get nervous. They want to know, "What about the thought that I had the other day—it was very negative. I watched that breast cancer infomercial and I really started to feel fear. Is that going to create breast cancer?" The answer is, of course not. Not unless all day, everyday, you are immersed in that state of fear.

Here's how it works. When you repeat the same thoughts and feelings over long periods of time, those thoughts and feelings become your beliefs. Think of such transient thoughts and feelings as being like water flowing along a constantly moving river. They'll move along with the flux of the river. It is not these transient thoughts but our belief systems that create our reality, so there's no need to fear those negative thoughts that seem to bounce around our heads every once in a while.

The fact is the Earth is a fear-based planet right now. All around you-on the TV or radio, in the newspapers, or in a conversation with your next-door neighbor—most of what you find is negative. It's a good idea to start to become aware of that negativity, and make choices that filter out as much of it as possible. What are you going to read? What will you watch on TV? Which people will you allow to be in your life? You are the only one who can take responsibility for those choices.

Once you start to embrace all this new information, which hopefully will become your new belief system, you will probably find that you want to maintain as much positive energy around you as possible. Your old life might seem to change because, as we stated earlier, when your frequency shifts everyone around you might start to shift as well. Some people will move closer because they see positive change in your life and they want to experience some of that positive change, too. Others may not be ready, and they might move away. These changes are nothing to be afraid of. Most human beings are inherently afraid of change, but when you look around our planet you'll find that everything in nature is constantly changing form. Change is wonderful—it is actually all there is. When we realize that, we can start to embrace change as an exciting adventure with positive expectations and a sense of joy. That's when the magic starts to happen.

✎ Exercise #16: Change is Wonderful—So Let's Create Some!

a. Choose a specific area of your life where you would like to create change, and write down your beliefs regarding that area.

b. Go back to exercise #3 and refresh your memory.

c. Based on your current beliefs, would the path you are now on get you to where you want to be?

d. In your journal, make two columns, with one column labeled "Negative Beliefs" and the other labeled "Positive Beliefs." In the Negative Beliefs column, write down the beliefs you found that were negative. Along with each of these, write out what you believe to be the origin of that belief. Did it originate with you, your mother, your father, a friend, one of your teachers, or some other source? On the opposite side rewrite these beliefs as positive.

As an example, you may be thinking, "I don't believe this information is going to help change my life in any way." Next to that, you might make the comment that this negative belief came from your father, who always questioned or even belittled everything you thought of. Then, in the positive column, write out your positive belief about the same issue: "I know this information is changing my life right now!"

e. Use these positive beliefs as affirmations. Affirmations are statements of truth. They are always in the now. It can never be tomorrow, because tomorrow is always out there; it never comes. Always state affirmations in a positive way. For example, you would never use the word never, as in, "I will never eat cheesecake again." Instead you would say, "I now eat fruit whenever I crave something sweet."

f. Repeat your affirmations each day, because the mind doesn't know the difference between real and make believe. After a short while your mind will actually believe your new positive affirmations, thereby allowing you to choose those behaviors that would be in alignment with your new beliefs!

g. What are the fear-based thoughts that run in your life?

h. What can you do to eliminate these?

i. What can you do to increase the positive in your life?

j. Make a list of the steps that you will take to accomplish this.

Responsibility

Another thing to talk about, while we are on the topic of creating our own realities, our belief systems and change, is "responsibility." I know that word can set off all kinds of anxiety. But let's take another look at it. As I'll be discussing it here, responsibility means being able to respond, in this case being able to respond to our own lives. To be *response-able* is to take back our power. Now doesn't that sound great? It's rather fascinating when you realize that throughout our lives we always have just one responsibility, whether we're five months old, five years old or fifty. That responsibility is simply to create our lives.

Creating your life is actually a very simple task when you understand and follow universal principle. However, with our need to feel in control, layered with all of the lies, denial and complexities that we humans seem to get lost in, we end up hiding our hearts, the gems of what's real. Notice how children's lives are filled with fun and joy, not because they have less responsibility but because they know the secret, the truth of who they are. Until the world takes that away with its programming, the joy remains, and so does their ability to respond.

When you think of your early concept of responsibility you may remember things that you didn't like to do but had to do anyway, like taking out the garbage or making your bed or cleaning your room. But back in those days, the worst that would happen if you didn't do those chores was probably that your mom or dad would nag you. However, in adult terms not taking responsibility, not responding to one's life, creates nothing. That is, if you choose not to take responsibility for your life, you'll find yourself just hanging around waiting to see what will fall to you by default. And by the way, that is a choice, as is everything.

The thing about choice is that it shows up everywhere in our lives. There are choices that we make consciously; those are easy to see. Like choosing to buy a new car, for instance. There are also choices that we would never dream we made, such as creating cancer, an automobile accident, a divorce or the loss of a job. And of course those choices, if we acknowledge them at all, may seem to have been made on an unconscious level—or so we would like to believe, since we would rather not take responsibility for creating realities that cause us pain or trouble!

There are some people who go so far as to argue that they have absolutely nothing to do with the difficult things that come into their lives, that those events were caused by someone else. We call that blame. We deny that we have anything to do with the problem and try to project it to "those other people or circumstances out there." This can even occur on a world wide level. In that case we call it "mass consciousness," with large portions of the population participating in denial. The end product is environmental pollution, wars, epidemics, economic disaster. Pretty amazing, isn't it! So if you want to help to change anything out there in the world, the best place to begin is with yourself. As we saw in the story of Marilyn and her husband, change has to start within.

It is difficult to think of the condition of the world as our responsibility, or that we could actually do something to improve things on that scale. No doubt your question is, "What can I do to change the world?" Here is the answer in an analogy: Think of a beach, a black beach, representing the state of our world right now. Most of us would rather imagine a beautiful white beach with a nice plush lounge chair, a sun umbrella, some nice music and maybe a *piña colada*. How can we change that black beach into the beautiful white sandy beach? The answer is, we do it one grain of sand at a time—or one person at a time.

If I pick up a grain of sand and hold it in the palm of my hand, I can't say that I have a beach in my hand. But I do have a part of that beach, and each part is exactly the same as every other part. Let's say that each one of us represents a grain of black sand on our beach. Now let's zoom in a little closer and see that one specific grain of sand that represents you.

After reading this book up to this point, your consciousness or frequency has already been raised, whether you're aware of it or not. Therefore that black grain of sand which represents you has now turned to dark gray, and with some more work it will become light gray and then white. Following that train of thought, as more people grow in consciousness and turn their little black grain of sand white, we will eventually change our entire beach from black to gray and then finally to white.

Taking responsibility at this level reminds me of Lauren Eisley's story about the starfish thrower. One day, while walking on the beach, a man notices that thousands of tiny starfish have washed up on the beach during the storm the night before. Those which weren't dying and rotting in the sun were being eaten by seagulls. But there in their midst was a man picking up the starfish one by one and throwing them back into the sea. The first man watched the starfish thrower for a moment, then asked, "What are you doing?"

"Throwing them back into the sea," the starfish thrower said.

"But it's so futile," the first man said. "It can't possibly make a difference."

Unperturbed, the starfish thrower picked up another fish and tossed it into the sea. "It matters to that one," he said, continuing to toss them back.

The starfish thrower took responsibility not for saving all the starfish but for doing what he was capable of doing. And that is all that any one of us needs to do.

I am going to give you an example now of the downside of responsibility as most of us would define it.

Ruby was 25 and still living with her parents. She started dating a lovely man who was well off and wanted to marry her. Under different circumstances I'm not quite sure that Ruby would have married but she did. Ruby was someone who wanted to be taken care of. The two were married and Ruby got everything that she had dreamed of—a huge engagement ring, a new home, a new car and a beautiful baby.

Then their financial situation began to deteriorate and her world fell apart. The first things to go were their leisure time activities, like expensive entertainment and frequent shopping trips. Next was her diamond ring, followed by their boat and the new car. Finally one morning my phone rang, and as I picked it up I heard screaming on the other end. When I was able to decipher the shrieks, what I heard was, "And now he's lost his job! Are you going to tell me I created that also?" and then slam went the receiver. I whispered into an empty phone, "Yes. I'm afraid it is only too true."

At times like these it is very difficult for people to understand why they would create such things. Why, as the title of the popular book seems to suggest, do Bad Things Happen to Good People? The truth is, there are no bad things and there are no good things. There are just things and what we do with them. Now, I'm quite sure that many people are going to object to this statement, but bear with me. When we can look at life this way, we can turn the worst things that happen in our lives into assets. We can often transform our worst nightmares by reminding ourselves of the old saying, "When life gives you lemons, make lemonade."

Clearly, in difficult times it's not that easy. However, that's what all this talk about responsibility is about—shifting your perspective. When you shift your perspective, instead of getting upset when bad things happen, you'll say, "There's some lesson I need to learn here. If I do, another door will open, allowing me a whole new view of life, with wonderful new opportunities." The good news is that, as you start incorporating this philosophy into the way you live each day, it will get easier and easier. It will become a part of who you are. It will make you response-able. I promise!

No matter what you might think, life does not have to be a struggle. Sometimes it seems that way because we were never given the tools that would allow us to be in an elegant flow of receiving. It's just not part of our consciousness. We believe we have to work hard if we want to be successful. You know, no pain no gain! That's the mentality that we live with. And guess what, believing makes it so.

✎ Exercise #17: Responsibility

a. Write down what your belief about responsibility is.

b. What were the first experiences of responsibility that you can remember and how did you feel about them?

c. Do your original feelings about responsibility have any effect on how you feel today? Explain.

d. What responsibilities do you feel you need to take on to change your life?

e. What would it take for you to be willing to accomplish that?

f. What choices (situations) do you have a problem believing that you created?

g. Since nothing can change till you do, either write out a statement or do a meditation taking responsibility for the above choices. Thank the universe and your higher self for the lesson(s) that those choices brought. If you have not learned the lesson(s) yet, ask for the understanding and clarity. Visualize what your life would be like once you've learned the lesson(s) and then surround those choices in white light, forgive yourself and release them, knowing that the change is occurring!

h. Go back to exercise #1, your victim story, and write out a new story, one in which you take responsibility for the event(s) and circumstances of that experience, and explain the lesson learned.

i. When you find yourself in situations wondering how you got into them, a good question to ask yourself is: what would a person have to believe about themselves in order to create a situation like that?

You may ask, "What about the starving children in Africa? Surely these innocents cannot be held responsible for their plight!" But perhaps they did choose this lifetime. They chose a lifetime of difficult and harsh service—in this case, to serve us by helping the world awaken to compassion. Hopefully, when enough people cannot bear to see other human beings living in cardboard boxes on a street, or the skeleton-like bodies of starving children, we will not allow it to happen anymore. And no, we are not going to walk up to those children and say, "Do you realize that you've created this reality for yourself?" We are going to feed them and help them to heal. Can we save them all? Perhaps not, but don't forget the parable of the starfish throwing.

Creating Versus Allowing

When we speak about creating our own reality, it's important to also address the issue of "allowing." In the above example I speak of a day when human beings no longer will allow children to starve. We have to face the fact that since we know that children are starving and yet the problem still goes on, then on a mass consciousness level we are allowing the problem to go on. We allow that situation into our reality for our own reasons, perhaps to support our belief that the world is a mess, or maybe to further our belief that, "There's not enough food for everyone." However, as long as we hold this problem in our minds without being response-able to it, the problem of starving children will continue, inviting us to learn some lesson. But what are the lessons? Maybe it's the lesson of compassion. Maybe it's the lesson of learning to act on our beliefs—to get involved with an organization that is working on that particular problem. Or maybe it's the lesson that we need to adopt a prosperity consciousness and not believe in lack. Whatever the reason, just be aware that if poverty and misery are in your reality, there is some lesson that you need to learn.

✎ Exercise #18: Allowing

What realities are you allowing and what are their lessons?

Programming

Some say that our society is made up mostly of human robots or "sheeple." I love that word! I first heard it from David Icke whose work, by the way, I list in the *Recommended Reading* section at the back of the book. He said that we are often like docile sheep allowing ourselves to be herded mindlessly through our lives, and that our planet is the way it is because *they*–the proverbial they–tell us what to do, how to do it, what to think, what to buy, and how to dress and look. Madison Avenue makes its billions because we remain *sheeple*. But Madison Avenue isn't alone by any means. Let's not even start on a discussion about government and our political leaders.

Now, please do not be offended; this is simply where we are now. The good news is that we're leaving this place and finding higher ground. We humans are equipped with the most incredible inner computers (our minds) that you can imagine, and we are little two-year-olds who simply have not learned how to use them yet.

A good analogy would be as follows: If I were to give my two year old niece the greatest computer in the world, it would be of little use to her because she doesn't know how to read the manual, and couldn't comprehend it even if she was able to read it. You and I know how to read, but our computers didn't come with manuals. The information about how to program our computers has literally been kept from us, keeping us in this robotic state. Robots are much easier to control! But the timing is right and we are ready, the earth is ready. (Actually she can't wait any longer.) And through our readiness we are creating the manuals and guide books. They are flowing in, from all directions. All we need now is the willingness to start reading and applying the information in our lives.

✎ Exercise #19: Rating Your Willingness to Change & Grow

What can you do to increase your level of willingness, so that you can find out who you really are and know what your fullest potential can be?

You come into this life with an unprogrammed computer. All you have is the basic hardware. Yes, I know about the past life stuff, that this may be part of our program. But for the sake of simplicity let's put that aside for now. That being so, let's begin when you're in your mother's womb. While there, all kinds of beliefs and perceptions about the world simply get programmed into your mind (computer). You soak them up by osmosis. One of the problems is that much of this information was actually programmed in by someone other than you—your parents or guardians, your teachers, your schools, mass media, etc. Once those beliefs are programmed in, they remain there until you become aware of them and choose to change them.

Do you ever wonder what you'll be like 10 or 20 years from now? Well, here's news; you'll be exactly as you are today, just 10 or 20 years older-unless you choose to change. And learning to change your programming is the key to making it happen. Boy, aren't you glad that you picked up this book!

Here's the good news. Now that we've begun to learn how to operate our computers we can take out or rewrite the old programs that prevent us from achieving what we want. That's responsibility at its best! We can install new programs that will create the lives that we desire! However, it does take effort. (I will not use the word "work" because of the way that word is programmed in us, and I do not want to find you hiding under the bed!) But making the effort is the most important thing that you can do for yourself. It will set you free!

✎ Exercise #20: Giving Back Beliefs That Were Never Yours

a. Go back to exercise #3 & #15, and look at all of the negative beliefs that hinder you in your life.

b. Write a letter to each of the people whose beliefs you accepted as your own. State that now that you realize these were never your beliefs to begin with, it is not appropriate for you to keep them any longer, for they are not in alignment with what you want to create in your life. You are now giving them back with your love and blessings. (Note: These letters are to be kept in your journal. They are written only for the people you still hold in your consciousness.)
c. Create a visualization for yourself, of the above story line.

Here's a point that's important to understand: Where assuming responsibility for your energy is concerned, it really doesn't matter if you're deaf, dumb, or blind. Everyone picks up energy! What I mean is this: You and your spouse are arguing and the children are around, so you motion to each other to go into the next room. Once there, you quietly fight so the children won't know about it. Well guess what? It doesn't matter where you fight because they are picking up your energy even when you are doing it in a locked, sound proof room.

I've often had clients who admit that they're in terrible relationships but they don't want to get divorced because of their children. I always tell them that if they are truly going to be responsible parents they need to know that their children are aware of what's going on, and they are being affected by it. By staying with the spouse in a bad situation, the parents are not fooling the kids; they are only fooling themselves. Do they really want to teach their children to stay in bad situations—because that is the lesson they are teaching. Perhaps the better lesson they might hand down is to be truthful. Come from their heart and don't allow a bad situation to continue.

✎ Exercise #21: Everyone Picks Up Energy

a. Are there circumstances in your life where others are picking up your energy, without you actually communicating to them?
b. If you could give up all of your fear, how would you handle this situation?

c. What would it take for you to give up your fear?

d. Bring the person that you need to speak with into your meditation and communicate everything with them there.

e. Send your higher self to their higher self.

f. Where has this happened in your past?

g. Having the knowledge you now have, through meditation, go back to the past event and change it.

Coming from Your Truth

When I speak about coming from your truth I am speaking about being true to yourself. In order to do that you must first understand who you are. What is your truth? So many of us were brought up in a way that actually prevents us from knowing who we are. We were taught that if we do spend any time getting to know ourselves, we are either day-dreaming or being self-centered. One of the things I recommend is for you to learn how to become intimate with yourself. A great way to do this is to be in touch with your thoughts and feelings throughout the day. Every now and then do a reality check—just check in and see what you are thinking and what you are feeling. Now don't laugh, I know it seems ridiculous, but you'll be amazed by what you'll discover this way.

Scientists say that the human mind thinks about 60,000 thoughts a day, or possibly more. Now tell me, do you remember the 60,000 thoughts you have during the course of any day? Clearly not! If you can think of 100 you're doing pretty well. So where are all those other thoughts? It's as though many of them are on a loop that plays continuously and repetitiously. What you'll find on this loop will be mostly fear-based and negative thoughts.

Even though we are not aware of why our thoughts and feelings keep plaguing us, they do, just like PMS, and I'm sure you guys who are reading this will bear witness to that! With all these negative thoughts running continuously through your head, you may feel like some zombie has possession of your mind, creating havoc on many different levels. You feel stressed, and your life begins to feel mediocre at best.

When you start to do reality checks, you begin to tune into the truth—your truth. You stop yourself at different times during the day and simply say, "Okay, what am I thinking and what am I feeling right now?"

You will slowly become conscious of the negativity and fear in many of those thoughts and feelings. What I want you to do at that moment is to stop. Change each of those thoughts and feelings 180 degrees; change them into positive versions on the same themes. The mind can only hold one thought at a time, so if you change to the positive, clearly you cannot be thinking the negative thought at the same time.

Learning to think positive thoughts is just strengthening a muscle. If you keep exercising the muscle it will grow in strength. If you exercise your mind to think positive thoughts it will eventually start doing that on its own. When you join the gym you do not walk out the first day in great shape. Only by working at it and strengthening those muscles will your body eventually look great. Well, this positive thinking muscle is the same.

By allowing ourselves to be conditioned by fear, instead of taking responsibility, we give away our power. We allow our polluted beliefs to create our reality. I'm not telling you that you have a terrible life. But no matter how good your life, believe me, it can get better. Once you take back your power and regain command of your life, you will start to learn a little bit more about who you really are. You will start seeing the puzzle of your life coming together in a way that makes perfect sense.

You will begin to look at your beliefs and question them. I would recommend that every few months, you look at any new beliefs that might have crept up on you. They are pesky little things. "Where do they come from?" you might ask. "Do they sneak up through the drain?" Sorry to say, the answer to that one is no. That would be too easy. The funny thing about beliefs is that when you start pulling them apart and taking a real good look at them, you might just find out that the life you have been leading until now wasn't even yours! Wow! Rather, you were accepting the *default settings* that life handed you. You had allowed these to determine who you are, your frequencies, without being response-able for checking them out and consciously choosing to keep them or change them. Until we take responsibility for our lives back, it is as if we are living our lives *possessed.* "Well if this isn't my life, whose is it!?" Indeed. Good question. Now think about that: You've been living your life based on someone else's thoughts and feelings. Talk about feeling foolish!

This is where the term *sheeple* comes in. As painful, or at least embarrassing as it might be, we have to ask ourselves who we want to be: Who are we? Do we really want to be free? If the answer is, "Yes, I want to be free!" then the only way to make that our reality is to actively pursue the task of finding out who we are.

To have the freedom you long for, you must have the courage to leave consensus reality behind, to leave the comfort of that mud puddle and stand in your circle of truth, that place where the only truth that prevails comes from your heart. When you find out who you are and what really matters to you, you can start creating beliefs in alignment with your truth and create the life of your choosing! How? Well, if you've gotten this far in the book you've made a good start. So read on. The best is yet to come.

Don't be overwhelmed! It's not unusual to feel this way when we discover how our beliefs create our reality, and that most of our beliefs were not even ours to begin with. But take heart. When you start to look at your beliefs, focus on the main ones that are giving you problems and handle them…one starfish at a time. Something miraculous will begin to happen as you join the endless flow of energy that our universe offers, not only dissolving problems that once seemed insurmountable but presenting you with exactly the choices you've been seeking to make your fondest dreams come true!

✎ Exercise #22: Checking In On Your Reality

a. Carry a notebook with you. Set up a schedule to do your reality checks and mark down all negative or fear based thoughts.

b. Change all negative and fear based thoughts to the positive.

c. Where do you act as a sheeple, not wanting to make waves?

d. What effect has it had on your life?

e. What would you do differently if it didn't matter to you what other people thought or said about you?

f. How would you do it differently?

g. What would it take for you to be willing to leave your little mud puddle?

Processing Questions

Use these questions to help you figure out your life puzzle.

1. What will it look like? (Physical description of what you want to create.)

2. What will it feel like? (Create an anchor of how you want to feel)

3. How will it change your life? This can be a biggy when you're trying to create something and it just doesn't seem to be happening. For example, Vickie wanted a new job. She did everything that a conscious person would do to create one and still nothing happened. She then answered this question. The answer was that she would have to give up all the time she now spent with her new boyfriend. Voila, there was the answer!

4. What will they say about it? (That's your sheeple question again.)

5. Why don't you want it? For everything that you want in your life, that you do not have, there is a reason you do not want it. We call this the payoff! Something like in #3, above, where Vickie was spending all her time with her new boyfriend.~

6: UNDERSTANDING YOUR FEELINGS

A very dear friend of mine was brought up by a mother who taught her children to never wear their hearts on their sleeves. The energy that went with those words was devastating: "Take your heart and bury it, so deep that no one can ever hurt it and no one can ever love it."

This friend is one of the most beautiful beings on the planet. Unfortunately, because of his mother's message he could never open his heart enough to be the least bit vulnerable. He could never allow another person access to feelings, thereby never creating a space for intimacy to grow.

This fear of being hurt is one of the reasons we humans are in such a sad state of affairs. Because we fear having our hearts broken, we settle for relationships, on all levels, where we think we are safe, never revealing the depth of our feelings, not even to ourselves. Our fear of being hurt keeps us from exploring our feelings about anything and everything. We live in a state of constant denial. (You remember, the 51st state!) This denial grows out of robotic programming, where we never question the beliefs that are passed along to us. Through this denial we create an absolute mess!

✎ Exercise #23: Understanding Your Feelings

a. What and when did the major hurts occur in your life?
b. How have they affected your life?
c: Do you allow intimacy in your relationships?
d. What is your fear now?
e. What do you need to do to overcome your fear?

Think of yourself as an iceberg. No, I am not just talking about being cold. The worst of it is that you're only aware of a small upper portion, the part you believe is safe to reveal. This top, tiny portion represents the feelings that you are aware of, and some of these feelings lead you around by the nose. (Maybe that's why some people have those nose rings these days?) However, who you truly are is way down below that. Remember, here as in nature the biggest part of the iceberg is way down below the surface. That's where you find your deepest emotions, which usually do not get addressed or even noticed because you have learned so well how to keep them hidden.

Most of us do not want to venture way down there below the surface because it's just too scary. It's the land of the unknown. We are afraid that the bogey man lives there, and everything we've every been taught says stay up here on the surface. Those who are a bit more conscious know that getting into one's emotions is the healthiest thing to do, though fear of the unknown still keeps most of us up there on the surface, playing in the nursery of life when it comes to our emotions.

Who knows what fears and secrets, what pains and heartaches we might discover down there! Who wants to just jump right in and possibly open Pandora's box? Or worse! Of course, what we do not realize is that down there in the shadows with all those fears, pains and ghastly skeletons, we also will find everything we have been longing for all of our lives—a depth of love, joy, spirituality and creativity, all just waiting to be discovered.

There is an NLP technique called anchoring, which allows you to access deep levels of wonderful emotions such as joy, love and fulfillment. (Review exercise #3 in your workbook.)

In working with many people around the discovery of their real depths, I have made some astonishing discoveries. For example, I recently asked a young woman to think back to a time when she felt a deep emotion. She thought about this for a long time. Finally she answered, "I don't think I ever have!" Unfortunately, this young woman is not alone.

It's heartbreaking to think of the levels of joy and love that are simply untouched by so many of us. You might be wondering why it is so easy to feel all those negative feelings, which sometimes burst to the surface and lead us around by the nose! The answer is that our feelings just emerge at whatever level of consciousness we live at. For example, most of us can easily remember times when we felt fear. That's absolutely no problem whatsoever. Since so many of us spend so much time in our "child" mode, (we will be exploring this in more detail soon) the feelings that surface are usually those of the "child," and that means we are feeling abandoned, embarrassed, not good enough, not loved and above all, frightened.

Given that you are in this state, it's easy to understand why your feelings might be so knee-jerk. Someone or something presses your button—or should I say your own inner child's or adolescence's button?—and then your feelings go off, you respond as the child, the adolescent, the victim, the martyr, and so on. All of these *personae* are part of who we are. When the child is in control, once again you, the adult, have lost the round! The good news is that you always have another go around, another opportunity to learn your lessons.

As you take care of business—your growth business—you will be able to move your conscious adult into the driver's seat and your buttons will not be nearly as easy to push. When they do get pushed, you will respond from a place of consciousness, of recognizing what is happening and of thereby being able to create a definite win for yourself. Your lesson is learned and so onto the next one, always progressing higher and higher!

So the answer is to never be afraid of your feelings, even though you might have to walk through the valley of the shadow, rubbing shoulders with the bogey man, right there where he lives. Keep in mind that it's simply a journey and that's why we're here, to explore this magnificent journey, to learn, grow and to find the magic and miracles along the way.

✎ Exercise #24: Titanic Revisited

a. What are the feelings beneath your iceberg?

b. What would make you feel safe enough to venture down there?

c. Create an anchor for the feelings that you have just described and get your scuba equipment on!

d. What are those fear-based feelings that lead you around by the nose?

e. Do these feelings remind you of your childhood?

f. Remember as far back as possible, to the first time you felt these fears.

g. What was going on at the time?

h. What are your buttons and who pushes them?

i. What feelings would you need to free you from reacting to these buttons?

j. Create a recipe anchor for the above feelings, with your anchor on visualize being in a situation that would normally push your buttons, however, you are now standing in your truth, with your anchor and you are not being affected!

You Are Not Alone!

After coming this far you might feel like you have as many questions as you have answers. But be patient with yourself. The search for answers is very much a part of this material. Look upon this journey as a mission— an important one. It is a challenge you took on before you even arrived on this planet, and that challenge is to help raise the consciousness of this planet, so that we can create change, magnificent change!

You see, you have a higher self—guides, Angels and teachers. These are already a part of your consciousness. As stated in Neal Donald Walsch's book, *Conversations With God*, they are "the grandest version of the greatest vision of you!" And that higher self has always been with you, for every lifetime. It always was and it always will be. It knows everything there is to know about you. If you want to know what you ate for breakfast ten years ago on the Fourth of July, just ask your higher self!

Your higher self knows exactly what you're doing in this lifetime, what your purposes are and what is the ultimate fulfillment that you can achieve. And they hang around patiently waiting for you to be ready to awaken to your destiny. They are the one's responsible for this book being in your hands. Whether it fell off the bookshelf or was given to you as a gift by your best friend, your higher self is the one who is responsible. When you show up some place you didn't expect to be, and it turns out to be something wonderful that you never would have thought of, that's the result of your higher self's efforts as well. They have your road map, which they constantly and gently offer to you, usually in whispers but sometimes they have to turn into screams when you are not willing to listen. One way or another, they gently nudge you with some good old-fashioned magic, and when you start to get it they are so excited! At this point they roll up their sleeves and the miracles begin.

You see most of the lifetimes they spend with you are pretty laid back, a lot of just rest and relaxation. However, some are about awakening and growth and that is most exciting to your higher self. And let me tell you, if you're reading this book the chances are pretty good that this is one of those lifetimes of growth. I think I can almost see your higher self jumping up and down with joy.

Once you start building a relationship with your higher self, the pieces of your puzzle start coming together rapidly. If you have ever done jigsaw puzzles you probably know how you always want to get the corners finished first, and then the borders. Imagine working on a puzzle of a forest and every piece of the puzzle is a leaf. Now, how frustrating is that! Well, that's what it's like to go through life not having a relationship with your higher self. Without your higher self it's as if you were doing a jigsaw puzzle where every piece looked the same and you couldn't even find the pieces that make up the corners and the borders.

Your higher self will start pointing out the corners and border pieces to you. Suddenly the picture of the puzzle, which is your life, starts to make sense, and from there on it's pretty clear sailing. Now that sounds pretty great, doesn't it? However, this is where you have to start consciously building a relationship with your higher self. You know what it's like when you meet a new friend and you discover that you two have a lot in common. There's this instant rapport, and you feel like you've known them forever! Well, even with this great rapport, if you only got to see them once a year your relationship with them would only be a fair one. If you saw that person every day, openly communicating and getting to know each other, you would have a great relationship going in no time. It's the same way with your higher self, especially in the beginning, as you build the relationship. Once your relationship is well established, and you feel the magic and empowerment of it, believe me you will not want to be without them. And you never will be as long as you do your best to maintain that relationship.

Best of all, you don't ever have to worry about being stood up or left waiting for hours! You can speak with your higher self just as you would speak with your best friend. For those of you who don't know what that's like it is simply opening your heart and communicating everything you're feeling—your desires (having nothing to do with genitals), your pain, your joy, your sorrows. You get it, right?

In the beginning most people communicate with their higher selves through meditation. As soon as you're comfortable, or even sooner if you like, you can communicate with your higher self anywhere, any time, because they are a part of you. Just be careful not to stand around in public places having loud conversations with them. There are some people who might not understand.

When you communicate with them, communicate from your heart. Let them know how grateful you are to have them in your life. Gratitude is a very important energy to work with. In fact, the more gratitude that you give the more that you will receive, which of course is not the only reason that you're doing it! Let them know that you realize you're new to all this, and you might need them to gently hit you on the head from time to time.

Realize that when you ask for answers, they can come from anywhere. They will not necessarily come from your higher self simply speaking to you, especially in the beginning. Do your best to let go of old feelings you might have such as whether or not you will be good enough or that help from your higher self just couldn't come in some of the forms that it will. Let me assure you that they will send you answers in ways you couldn't possibly imagine. Books fall from shelves, you bump into strangers who just happen to have an answer that you've been looking for, a piece of newspaper falls to the floor opening to a page that tells you exactly what you needed to know at that moment, and so forth. Simple magic! And, oh yes, if you are having trouble accepting that all this can really be true, don't hesitate to ask your higher self to help you to be more willing to receive their guidance.

One of our biggest blockages is simply not being willing to receive, and that goes for every area of our life. This again comes from our earliest programming—our belief in lack, that there's never enough to go around, and our belief that we're not good enough, or that it can't happen this easily because there has to be some struggle...and so on. You know all the doubts and fears that run around in your brain.

Once you've communicated with your higher self and you feel you have given all your questions over to them, and have explained exactly what you want to create, simply go along your own way, knowing that all is taken care of and that the answers will come. Your heart's desire will be fulfilled!

Be aware and alert now, because sometimes what we want comes to us in different packages than we are expecting! You see, years ago we all decided what it was we wanted when we grew up, and we created the pictures to go along with those dreams. Now, years later, most of us still have those same pictures. In some cases it might still work. Let's say success for you back then was getting married, having your children and being a housewife. Then you grew up. Women's Lib came along and you decided you wanted a great career in advertising.

You might still be struggling in this career, wondering why it isn't working, when in actuality your inner loop of beliefs, which you formed in childhood, is still running. This part of you believes that what you want is still to be a housewife taking care of your little nest and your children.

Each time you venture out to make your dream career a reality, you end up sabotaging your chances because your old beliefs are still on that loop

✎ Exercise #25: You Are Not Alone—So Start Working!

a. Write a letter to your higher self, thanking it for all that it's done for you. Tell it what you would like to create with it now.

b. Higher Self Meditation: Close your eyes and go into a meditation, relaxing your body and mind and finding your way to a safe and beautiful place in nature. Visualize a bright white light coming down from the universe towards you. Bring it in right in front of you. This is your higher self. Ask for its name. The first name that comes to your mind is it. Now sit down and start communicating with it. At any time your higher self might take on a human form and that's fine. Just allow it to be what ever it is! Visit with your higher self everyday and you'll have a wonderful relationship.

c. What were your old pictures of success?

d. Create your new pictures of success. (Refer back to the processing questions in exercise #22 if you need help.)

Highest Good

I'm sure you are familiar with the saying, "Be careful of what you ask for you will surely get it!" Well, that's where your highest good comes in. It's like a spiritual security blanket. Anything intended for your highest good is in the highest order for your life. As such, it is something the Angels would smile upon, and so does your higher self. While you might want something to happen in your life, and feel pretty sure it's right for you, your higher self just might have something better planned for you. Clearly they know better than we do, though I realize there are people who believe that they know better than their higher self and God/Goddess.

When we're not working with our higher self and allowing ourselves to honor its guidance, we usually end up going 100 miles out of our way. Our highest good is always the shortest route between any two points, the points being where you are now and where your fullest potential lies, which just happens to be where your higher self wants you to be! Remember your higher self always knows what destiny you are here to fulfill, and they will try to get you there, if you are willing. I'll explain it with a story.

Once upon a time there was a young artist named Becky living in New York City. Unfortunately she was not able to sell much of her work, so she painted by day and was a waitress by night to pay the bills. Becky's two best friends had both left New York: one got married and moved to Oshkosh, the other moved out to Santa Fe to explore a more spiritual life, something that had intrigued our friend Becky. Well, it was Becky's birthday and both friends wanted to spend time with her.

Becky had a decision to make. She loved both of her friends but suburban life in Oshkosh was not as exciting as going out to Santa Fe. Becky had been reading some books on metaphysics and had learned about highest good. She had made a commitment to herself. She would always try to be consciously aware of her life. At this moment, with the decision of her trip on her mind, she decided to go into a little meditation. She asked her higher self for some clarity. What was it to be, Oshkosh or Santa Fe?

When Becky came out of meditation she went about her day knowing that within the next few days the answer would become clear. Sure enough, the next day as Becky was sitting and waiting for her laundry, one of those things that she tried to get her higher self to do for her, but to no avail! The guy sitting next to her dropped a map on the floor and as Becky reached over to pick it up for him, she noticed a red circle around Oshkosh. Becky handed the map back to the guy and asked if he was going there. He immediately started telling her all about Oshkosh, which just happened to be the town where he grew up.

As Becky left the Laundromat she was quite sure the decision was now clear. Although she was a little disappointed that she would not get to see Santa Fe, she realized that if this was for her highest good there must be some reason she was being guided there. To make a long story short Becky did pack up and head out to Oshkosh. After three days she was quite ready to go home, and was wondering what her higher self might have been thinking to arrange this trip. Temporary insanity was the first thing that came to Becky's mind!

On the fourth day all packed, suitcase at the door and saying her good-byes, there was a knock at the door and Becky went to answer it. The woman standing there introduced herself as the sister of the next-door neighbor. She said she had just arrived from New York City. The woman had come to ask Becky's friends if they had a corkscrew that she could borrow. As Becky's friend went to search, Becky and the woman from New York started up a conversation and as it turned out the woman owned an art gallery in SoHo and was looking for new work to show!

Need I say more! Highest good in action! If Becky had not committed herself to live consciously, she simply would have gone to Santa Fe, where she probably would've had a better time, but it would not have been for her highest good. Her artwork is her purpose and service here in this lifetime, and upon following that path Becky has become financially abundant.

When we live life consciously, ask for our highest good and are willing to receive it, we save time and mileage, for opportunities will keep coming till we are ready to receive. The old saying that opportunity only knocks once is false. It will keep knocking until you are ready to receive. The question you might ask yourself is why not receive now? Remember we can save ourselves from some of the traumatic lessons of reality by asking for our highest good always to be revealed to us. Sometimes we simply make stupid choices on our own. Ask and you shall receive!

✎ Exercise #26: Your Highest Good

a. Can you think of a time that you were detoured on your journey because you were not open to your highest good? Explain b. Do a meditation with your higher self. Explain that you are ready and willing to receive your highest good, ask for your higher self's guidance and give your gratitude for it already happening.

Let Your Higher Self Work for You

You can send your higher self to the higher self of anyone you have a problem with, whether it's your spouse, a parent, your boss, or the person that you might have a crush on. Clearly these guys can handle it much better than we ever could, especially when our childish or adolescent beliefs get involved!

Simply tell your higher self what the problem is, how you feel about it, your fears, your goals, and then simply ask them to work it out with the other person's higher self. Let me tell you another story.

John had always missed the nurturing of his mother, for she was a very cold woman and was never able to show her love. She had two grown children in their 50s and she had never hugged them or said that she loved them. Even though John was in his 50s there was still that part of him, that child within him that still wanted mommy's love!

After John learned about using his higher self to do his work he explained the situation to his higher self. He also visualized his mother surrounded with pink light, which is the light of love, in his meditations. At Christmas, John went home as usual, and to his surprise, when his mother came to the door she flung her arms around him and gave him the biggest hug he had ever had as she whispered I love you!

This is powerful stuff! You can also send your higher self ahead to create a path for you in a new opportunity, such as a job interview or a new relationship. Always remember to ask for the highest good of all involved. Here's an example. Laura was going for a job interview and was very nervous because she hadn't worked in years. She was going through a divorce and the job meant a lot to her and her children. Laura told her higher self everything that she was feeling; she also included the name of the person she was interviewing with and the salary that she needed to receive.

Laura hadn't typed in years, let alone used a computer, so one of her main concerns was what would happen if they asked her to take a test. When the big day came she anchored in her courage and went on the interview. Everything was going very well. Laura and the woman giving the interview connected very nicely. Then all of a sudden the woman said all that was needed now was for Laura to take a simple test on the computer. At this point Laura froze. The woman buzzed her receptionist to come and take Laura to the room where she'd be tested. However, the receptionist miraculously wasn't there! After waiting a few more minutes the woman said to Laura, "Well, I guess it's not really that important. If you'd like you can start on Monday!" Over the weekend, Laura brushed up on her typing and had a friend give her a crash course on the computer. The following week work went perfectly.

The ways of magic! At this point you have a pretty good idea of how to work with your higher self. Just remember, the more you work with them the more intimate the relationship will be. You can even take them to the movies with you. However, if someone should ask if the seat next to you is empty, "No, my higher self is sitting there," would not be a good answer! The good news is they don't even need a seat or a ticket!

✎ Exercise #27: Let Your Higher Self Do the Work for You!

Make a list of those things, which you would like your higher self to co-create with you. In meditation let your higher self know what needs to be done.

Our Other Unseen Friends

Besides your higher self you have guides, angels and teachers to help you. If you could only see the magnitude of guidance and support that surrounds you, you would not only be shocked but you would never feel fear again. Any task that you do, you can assign a guide, I have a guide of the road whose name is Leo. He keeps me focused so I can make the correct turns and get off highways at the right exits because I have a tendency to space out when I'm driving. If I forget to ask Leo to guide me, I could be 20 miles up the highway before I realized I missed my turnoff.

Before I start off on my trip I simply ask Leo to inform me five minutes before my exit, and it's done. Just about five minutes before my exit, my awareness comes right back to where it needs to be, and I simply move over to the lane where I need to exit.

You can have guides for anything that you do and want to do better. How about an accountant guide to nudge you when you're about to max out your Visa card, or a kitchen angel so you don't burn the tofu when the in-laws come to dinner. Be as creative as possible and watch the difference. You will be an amazed!

Remember; always give gratitude for all of your guides' assistance. ~

✎ Exercise #28: Your Unseen Friends

a: Decide which specific areas of your life you would like to have guides for, and bring them in the same way you did for your higher self. Call them in to help you before starting any project. The more you work with them, the easier it will be to see the magic they are creating.

b. Write a letter to each of your guides, telling them what you want to create with their assistance, and explain the tasks you want them to perform. ~

7: Change Bodies and Dance

Fasten your seats belts, we don't want to lose anyone! We spoke before about energy and how it cannot be destroyed: it simply changes form. And since the form we are now speaking of is our physical bodies, guess what? That means we are going to be talking about reincarnation! So let's look at it this way: yes, reincarnation is real. Okay, that's that! We're finished! Let's get on to the next chapter. Actually, I'm just kidding. But the truth is that every holy book ever written speaks or, at least, originally spoke of reincarnation. The only thing is, it was either edited out or through translation ended up having a different meaning. Hmm, I wonder how that might have happened. Could it have anything to do with political or religious control?

Getting on with our story, think of it this way: You're 105 years old. You've had a great life and now you're ready to leave. Let's not try to kid anyone, after 105 years your body is not what it used to be! You can't go bungee jumping any more, and staying out until three in the morning just doesn't cut it either. So it's time to trade in the old body. You have no problem when your car gets old and worn out. You trade it in and get a new one. Well, it's basically the same thing here.

So, it's late at night and you're in your bed. You close your eyes and notice a beautiful white light in front of you. The light is so alluring and so beautiful! The closer it gets the more at peace you feel. Because you are a very conscious human being and you've been working on yourself for some time, you realize it's time to change bodies. You just surrender to the peace—actually you're quite excited about what lies ahead. You finally will find out the truth. Everything you have been studying and wanting to know more about will finally be revealed. It is about to become your one and only reality, the only real reality there is!

Next scene: You are here in what has been called the afterlife or heaven. Everyone here simply refers to it as "home," or "home base," because this is where we all start from and where you always return to. Here you are met by your higher self and it's where you begin the process of planning for the next lifetime. Yes, there are options: if you feel like you need a rest—and after a lifetime on Earth, I certainly think you might need one—you can simply become one with all that is, or God energy, and just hang out. Don't worry about your wardrobe. Here everything is simply energy. (Remember the movie *Cocoon?*)

There's a second option, of course. Let's say you are ready and willing to go back to Earth and do it again. Hopefully this time you're going to do it on a higher consciousness level. You'll be choosing new lessons, which means that you learned most of your lessons in the life you just left.

Want still another option? Maybe, just maybe, you are ready to graduate from planet Earth, never to go back there again because you have learned everything there is to learn back there. It's time to move on to other levels of reality—and by the way there are many! But that's the subject for another book.

Moving right along…let's say you choose to go back to Earth, you brave soul you! This is where you and your higher self start to work. You are going to be setting up the plans for your next journey to Earth. Think of it like this: remember when you were in high school and every year you would have to go to the guidance counselor to prepare for next year's schedule? You would sit down with the counselor who would then explain that in order to graduate you would have to complete a specific curriculum. You would go over those classes that you had already taken—let's say English 1, Geometry, Earth Sciences, etc. Your counselor would then explain that you would now have to take English 2, Trigonometry, and Chemistry. These classes were required for your graduation. Well, it works pretty much the same at *home.*

As you've already learned, your higher self has the ability to know everything about you, from every one of your lifetimes—what lessons you have completed and which ones you still need to complete in order to graduate from planet Earth. Now, you might be asking why you would want to graduate from planet Earth. Why wouldn't you want to come back? The answer is simple: So many places to go to, so many new realities to experience!

Okay, let's recap here: you've left your body back on planet Earth because you wanted one of those newer models. So here you are with your higher self on that plane of reality we will call home. Both you and your higher self have just been going over all of your past lives to see which lessons you have learned and which ones you still need to learn. In between a cup of carrot juice and a veggie burger, your higher self shows you that in past lives you have learned about humility, creativity, becoming financially independent, and loving others. However, there is one area that seems to have caused you considerable problems in these lifetimes. The fact is that you often felt you were not good enough. You're not alone in that one, believe me! It's a problem that many humans share.

So, it is decided that the main lesson you'll be going after in your upcoming life is *learning that you are good enough.* As you announce this to your friends around home base, there is a loud roar of applause…you see, I told you it was a problem many humans share! And now that you have the focus of your upcoming life, you will now start creating your script for the next adventure back on planet Earth.

✎ Exercise #29: Your Life Lesson

Write out what you believe your lessons are for this lifetime.

Remember, it's all a movie!

Did you ever wish you could be a movie star? Well most of us, at one time or another have had that wish, and I'm sure you will be glad to know that your wish has now been granted. But then, you have been one all along. You just didn't realize it. Our planet serves as the largest theater in the galaxy. Each one of us has a vast repertoire, and each part we play contains a lesson which, when learned, rewards us with a gift. But please don't be expecting a free three-day getaway to Hawaii. Not only are you the actor/actress, you are also the screenwriter, the director, the producer, the set designer, the fashion designer, and the casting agent. Talk about power!

The upcoming show is all yours, just as all the past ones were. You will write the script, design the set and the props. You will choose the fashions and all the characters. You will have it all worked out—with the help of your higher self—way before you get back to your new life on Earth.

Now please understand, the Earth is a free will zone, which basically means that you can create anything you want, and I mean anything. God/Goddess does not judge you, nor is there right or wrong in God's eyes, as I explained in the opening statement to this book about God/goddess.

Back to the writing of your script: In order for you to learn something new, there has to be a point in time that you did not know this something. Right? So if you are coming into this new lifetime and your lesson is to learn that you are good enough, you must start out thinking that you're not good enough. Now, let's not get overwhelmed here. We're going to do everything in little baby steps. And the first of the steps is that we have to agree that you need to start out somehow—in this case with the feeling that you're not good enough. How are you going to accomplish this? Well, you and your higher self decide that you will come into this life with parents who will be great at teaching you to feel that you're not good enough. But parents are not all you'll need. You will also create the rest of the script, with events and characters who will be just perfect for showing you that your belief of not being good enough is true. Why do you need all these people to substantiate your feelings? Because we always like to be right—even when we are wrong! Thus, you'll be starting from this place of feeling not good enough, having people around who will back you up on that feeling, and then what? Then you will stay that way until you choose to change it. But don't despair because your higher self is always aware of your purpose in each lifetime. They are always aware of the highest potential you can achieve, and they will always guide you in that direction.

Remember, as you consider all this, that Earth is a free will zone, and you are always making choices here. Here's a comparison to think about: There are books and computer games that allow you to make choices as you're playing along. The choices will create different endings to the storyline. This life script that you are working on back at home base is the same way. At different times in your life you will find yourself at junction points where you will have the opportunity to make different choices. There may be two or more paths you can take, each choice creating a different set of probable realities. Probable, because you have many possibilities for many lives out there, just as with the computer game. These different choices and different lives literally do exist. You will create one of them based on your choices, choices created by the level of consciousness at which you are functioning at any given time.

Keeping all this information about choices in mind, and getting back to our story, you can understand why this script that you and your higher self are writing can only be a loose version at best, because in real life—that is, life back here on planet Earth—you are always making choices that can change your outcome. That, in fact, is a big part of what we are supposed to be learning back here on our temporary home planet. Here are some points to understand:

1. Time is simultaneous, and everything that has ever happened has happened already. This is one of those topics that could make your brain fry, like a piece of fried chicken, extra crispy. To make it painless, think of a film that's being delivered to a movie theater: the whole movie is already right there on the film, from the beginning to the end. However, as you sit in the movie theater watching the movie you are still quite excited because you do not know how the movie is going to turn out—even though it is right there on the film all along. Everything that has ever happened or ever will happen is going on right now. It simply depends where you're focusing. We happen to be focused in this new millennium. If we choose

to, we can focus on any time, in any of our lives. And the vehicle we would use to get there would be meditation.

2. Although you create your own script and cast your characters before you can come back to this planet, you still have free choice, you can still choose again, any moment during your life on Earth.

3. You always know what you have chosen. At some level of consciousness, you will know what script you chose back on home base, and you will know the choices you have made here on planet Earth. You may not be easily able to access this information, in order to remember these choices, but if you fully recognize the realities discussed above in #1, you will quickly recognize that this is true.

Okay, at this point I can hear the brain frying process going on. Relax. Know that you may not fully grasp the above three concepts initially but all you really have to do is load it into your computer (your brain) and let it go. Don't try to understand it or fully believe it. Your brain will play with these ideas automatically, and when you finally need them they will be there ready for you. You might consider rereading this book, or portions of it, from time to time and all the ideas will eventually come together. Also check out "recommended reading" at the end of the book.

Now that you have created your life script, we are ready to look at....

✎ Exercise #30: Your Life Script

Write out what you believe your life script has been up to this point.

The Process of Casting Your Script!

We all have a soul group, or spirit family, that we belong to, and we always stick together. Think of it as being like a summer stock theater group, traveling from city to city performing their plays. There will always be the same cast members but in each play they may take on different roles. For instance in one play, Dawn might be the wife and Tom the husband; in the next Tom might be the father and Dawn the next-door neighbor. Yes, in our life scripts we get to switch genders from time to time. (And sometimes we forget that we actually switched!)

As your little repertory group moves from city to city, or lifetime to lifetime, as the case may be, some cast members might decide to take a short break. In other words, the group might be going to New York but Dawn and Tom need a rest, so they go their own way and will meet up again with the rest of the cast at the next stop in Philadelphia. So, if you're ever walking down the street and you happen to notice a familiar face, it's probably one of your soul group that you will not be hooking up with in this lifetime. It's just that you both decided to just stop for a moment and say hi. And, of course, those *deja vu* kinds of feelings that you have with some people, where you feel as if you have known them for years, is simply because you probably have shared many lifetimes together.

The important thing to understand here is that this soul group is formed in pure love. Moreover, these beings, and all beings, are pure light, and will always be in that place that we call home with God/Goddess. How can they always be at home, you might ask, if they are out having lifetimes with me and other members of my soul group? The five million dollar answer is that as light beings we can be in more than one place at a time. In the time-space dimensions where light beings exist there is no linear reality as we understand it here on Earth. This is a good time for a story.

Scene 1: While Ellen and David were married, nothing ever went smoothly. They'd been drawn together by lust at first sight. There were no grounds for friendship and so the rest was downhill all the way. Ellen had grown up in a very dysfunctional home, where love meant being abused. And just as we have learned, Ellen created the same kind of marriage with David: screaming, yelling and a slap across the face would send Ellen fleeing to her room, only to remember the same nightmares of her childhood.

Along the way Ellen learned to make better choices and finally divorced David. And even though Ellen did change her life for the better, she was never really able to release the anger and hurt that she had towards David.

Years later, David ended up getting help. He came to visit Ellen to ask for forgiveness, however, Ellen was simply not able to forgive. Holding in all that anger and hurt eventually caused her to die of cancer at an early age. David came to visit her when she was in the hospital and even then she couldn't forgive him.

Scene 2: We are now back at home base, bathed in the Divine Light of God/Goddess. We see two light beings approaching one another. They are old and dear friends. They embrace and then we hear this conversation:

"It's so good to be back home isn't it? Boy, didn't we have fun in that last lifetime down on Earth! You certainly played a great tyrant. Your screaming and yelling was incredible. You deserve an Oscar."

"Well, you were great too. The way you used to run into your room, I thought that one day you would come hurtling out and hit me over the head. You know what? We had so much fun with those roles, how about going back again, only this time I'll be the husband and you be the wife."

The two old friends shake on this, hug once again, and walk into the Divine Light from which they came, the best of friends, forever!

Now this is crucial for you to understand: your soul group is your family, your best friends. You are all there to love and support each other at all times, including those times when you are playing roles together during one of your lifetimes down on Earth. It does not matter if they show up in a lifetime to kill you, beat you, or do any other horrendous things. Their real purpose is to always be there to love and support you in any choice that you might make for a particular lifetime. They are there to help you learn whatever lessons you need to learn. Also remember that you were the casting agent that signed them on for their roles. Let's see what that looks like.

Casting Call!

Now that you understand you have a soul family that is always together, and that light beings can be in more than one place at a time, you can also understand why they are always at home when you get there.

Similarly, when you are ready to choose another lifetime on planet Earth, they will be ready for the casting call. Here is how it's done:

Your higher self and you, with scripts in hand for your upcoming life, will meet with your soul group. The members of your soul group also have their scripts in hand, for their upcoming lives. You start by explaining the characters that you need for your upcoming life.

Let's say you start with your mother. You explain that you need a mother who somehow will teach you that you're not good enough. Possibly she will always be there to tell you that you're not cleaning up your room good enough or you're not pretty enough or you're not smart enough, and so on. Very quickly, your soul group gets the picture. Each of them now looks at their scripts to see if your role fits into theirs. One of the beings in the group starts jumping up and down with excitement, saying the role is just great for her. It is going to fit into her script perfectly!

There are always mutual needs that get fulfilled in these cast calls. For example, in the personal script chosen by the woman who is going to play your mother, there is a need for a daughter just like you are going to be—someone with low self-esteem issues who they can always be controlling and showing she's not good enough. You both run up to each other, hug, and then shake on it. It's a deal! You will meet each other in the upcoming life and will play out your scripts. It's perfect.

You then proceed through all the characters the same way, until you have everything you need for your next stint on Earth.

Now you're ready to create, your gender, race, health condition, and financial status. Also the choice of the set design—the physical environment where you live, which includes the actual year, the political milieu, the country, the city, the town, the actual house, apartment, or cardboard box where you'll live. Next would be the fashion design, and the image that you'll portray. Will you be fat or thin, beautiful or homely or something in between?

At this point you might be thinking, "Why, in heaven's name, with all this power, would I choose a lifetime where I would be ill or fat or homely or living in horrific times of social oppression?" I'd much rather just be beautiful, wealthy, healthy, and living in Paris. And the answer is, as a conscious being, which you are, when you're making these plans from home you realize that each lifetime is simply the blink of an eye, in all of eternity—and you have all of eternity. So it doesn't really matter what you choose, except that this choice will fulfill a need. Remember the analogy of sitting down with your academic counselor and deciding which classes you needed for graduation? It's like that. Keep in mind, though, that it is all an illusion anyway, a concoction of light and sound. When it's put together it will seem totally real.

Here's a good clue to understand why sometimes, life on Earth seems so frustrating and overwhelming. When we are making our choices of script and cast, just before we come into a lifetime, we are just as God/Goddess is, that is, omnipotent, omnipresent, and omniscient. And from that standpoint, when we think of a life on Earth, well, that would be a breeze. There's nothing we cannot accomplish. However, we don't realize that when we get into our physical bodies, that's when the problems begin. Guess what? The minute we enter our physical bodies, we develop total amnesia about who we really are, which strips us of our power…until we start remembering!

Hang in there! We've almost got it together. We have our script, our characters, the set design, and the fashion design, and of course we have our higher self, as always. So, what's next?

✎ Exercise #31: Casting Your Script

Using the script you wrote up in Exercise #30 as your guide, do the following:
a. Explain why you believe you chose the main characters you did in your script.
b. Describe each lesson that the above characters have taught you, or is teaching you.
c. Ask yourself if the lessons you are to learn are completed, or if you have more to learn.

d. Is there anything you would change in your fashion or set design?

Lights-Camera-Action...

Now that you have a great understanding of all this creation stuff, let me show you how it works. I'd like to introduce you to Mindy. As we join her, Mindy has just completed all the work necessary to begin a new life here on planet Earth. She has her script, her main life lesson, which will be the same as we discussed earlier: learning to feel good enough. She also has chosen her cast of characters and everything else that goes with the show. And, oh, yes, about now she is in her mother's womb!

Now, before we go on I want to remind you that in order for Mindy to learn that she is good enough, she must start out feeling *not good enough*.

As our story begins, Mindy is curled up in her mother's womb. She is aware of everything that is going on in her environment. Her computer is on, picking up all energy which will create Mindy's first beliefs. Here is the main theme of what she has already heard and recorded in her memory banks: Upon learning that his wife is pregnant Mindy's dad-to-be bellows at her mom: "I told you not to get pregnant. We haven't got enough money for that. And besides, I don't want that kid!"

So Mindy gets born. It's not a great experience for her. Her mother, who is not at all happy with the whole situation, tenses up and makes the whole birthing process a nightmare.

Finally out of the womb, through only minimal help on Mom's part, the doctor places little Mindy on her mother's chest. Mom takes one look at her, makes an unpleasant face and says to the nurse, "Gee, she's pretty funny looking. Are you sure she came out of me?" She hands the baby back to the nurse.

All of this goes right into Mindy's computer. She is off to a roaring good start in fulfilling her chosen script that she is not good enough.

Life goes on, pretty much as you might guess, with Mom doing her motherly duties through gritted teeth. Mindy is almost five years old and her mother has insisted that she is now old enough to do her hair by herself. Mindy gives it a valiant try, racing downstairs all excited about showing off her new hairdo which she created all by herself.

Her mother meets her with her hands on her hips, squinching her face up like there was a bad smell in the room. Her response shatters poor Mindy: "You look terrible, even worse than when you were born. Go back upstairs and do it right."

When her friends come over to play, somehow they always end up hurting Mindy's feelings. She frequently runs to her room, feeling, of course, not good enough. It is plain to see that Mindy's computer is now filled with all those not-good-enough beliefs, with all those little magnets going out into the universe, pulling in a string of events in physical reality to match Mindy's beliefs about herself.

Mindy is starting school. She lives in the small town and there are only two kindergarten teachers, Mrs. White and Mrs. Black. Mrs. White is a wonderful teacher, the kind of teacher that if a child painted a tree that was purple and pink, she would say, "Oh, how absolutely wonderful and creative. I think you're going to be another Picasso!"

Mrs. Black, on the other hand, came from quite a dysfunctional family, with her own low self-esteem programming. If that same child came to Mrs. Black with that purple and pink tree, her response would be, "What's that supposed to be?! I never saw such a tree in my life! You go right back to your desk and paint a tree the way it is supposed to look!"

Keeping in mind that we each create our realities based on our beliefs, which teacher do you think Mindy will bring into her life? Correct! Mrs. Black. After Mrs. Black there will be boyfriends who criticize Mindy for not being pretty enough, and bosses who complain she is not fast enough or thorough enough, no matter how well or fast she works.

If you are like most people, I'm pretty sure you are asking how it is possible that Mindy would only create all of those negative situations in her life? And the answer is she wouldn't. There would also be many positive people, who would tell her that she's pretty and wonderful. The problem is she wouldn't believe them, because she would have no place where that kind of feedback would fit. This is how it will go for the rest of Mindy's life. And should I remind you that if you want to know what you'll be like ten or twenty years from now, you'll be the same as you are now, only ten or twenty years older!

So, unless Mindy chooses to change, things are going to be pretty much the same for the rest of her life. That's a pretty grim picture and rather sad. However, let's not overlook that one little phrase…*unless Mindy chooses to change.* Yes, we now have the knowledge to change and it's spreading like wild flowers!

Now before we say goodbye to Mindy, she wants to show you one more thing, her x-rays. At midlife she began learning all about all these things we've been talking about here. She was so determined to change her beliefs that she started playing detective to find out what beliefs she held in each area of her life. Here are her results:

* Heart Area: This is the center of her self-esteem issues, her not-good-enough stuff. The color or frequency is brown.

* Career Area: If you have tuned in on Mindy's life, you know this area can't be a very high frequency since low self-esteem hits this area particularly hard. Even if she was making a million dollars a year and getting awards right and left, she would probably still be feeling like she was not enough. So this area matches her heart area: brown.

* Health. In spite of herself, Mindy enjoyed pretty good health, so her color and frequency there were in the red area.

* Relationship. Mindy is back to dark blues and dark greens here. Most of her relationships have just reinforced her not-enough feelings, but lately she has been able to enjoy some very positive people, too.

* Fun. Hmm. A month ago Mindy would have asked, "What's that?" Lately, though, she has been meeting a friend every Friday for lunch at a great restaurant. They met in a spirituality workshop and they love talking about all these exciting ideas that are so new to them. Bright blues are coming into her aura in this area.

* Spirituality. For some reason—maybe it's because her higher self keeps checking in—her frequency has always been very high in this area: bright yellow.

* Creativity. Thanks to Mrs. Black, the kindergarten teacher she had way back when, Mindy has always thought of herself as having about as much creativity as a banana. In fact, she would have represented her frequency as having about the same colors as a slug. Lately, though, she has been writing private poetry and some of it is darn good. So she rates herself medium high here, with an emerald green color.

* Intellect. Although Mindy drew people into her life who reinforced her not-enough image of herself most of the time, she had always enjoyed intellectual challenges. Besides, intelligence tests in school always rated her high, something her mother occasionally bragged about to her friends. So in this area, Mindy gave herself a medium high rating, in the color range of orange.

Having a different frequency and color in each area indicates that life isn't all...well...black and white. For instance: although you might generally feel not good enough, you could enjoy good health, have a highly successful career, and be a creative person. Another person could feel that she was *not good enough,* might have poor health, and always be in financial difficulties but still have a great relationship. It depends on where you allow your *stuff* to affect your life.

✎ Exercise #32: Your Beliefs

Go over Exercise #14 and see if there is anything you'd add.

Give Yourself a Shot at an Oscar!

The show is all yours, you wrote your script! Most of us walk around clutching that same dog-eared, coffee-stained script all our lives, never realizing that we are its author. You always were and always will be.

But…just as you wrote that script you can also rewrite it. Just do the work. Deci
what you need to change and change it! When you're watching a horror video
your VCR and you don't like it, hopefully you have enough sense to push the ej
button. It really can be as simple as that.

And, oh yes, if you're wondering who the idiot was who cast those other idi
who keep lousing up your movie, walk directly to the mirror and say hello. Clear
it was a joint decision, that is, you chose them to be part of your cast because the
was a lesson that you needed them to teach you…and they had their lessons whi
fit you like a glove. You don't remember right now because you are immersed
living your script. But way back at home base, last time around, you shook on it a
agreed that you would play out this script together.

If all this is starting to get painfully clear, don't fret. Remember, you are rewriti
your script. As you do this, you might find that there are some actors in yo
present script who will change in an instant, almost as if by magic, when you st
casting your new roles. As for the rest, you can give them their walking papers! Th
will have to go off and find someone with a script where they have a role to play.

Are you worried that once you change the script you won't have anyone arou
you? Forget that! There will always be people in the wings just waiting to be broug
in. So remember to be very careful about what you ask for and who you ask it
And don't forget to ask because you might get it!

The same thing goes for the set and fashion design departments. You're the bo
If something is wrong, such as, you're living in a shack and would like a mansion,
you are fat and want to be thin, remember you can change it. It's all an illusion, ju
like Hollywood. Your mind is creating it all based on what your thoughts a
feelings are and what you are willing to receive. Be honest enough to admit th
your movie is a flop, change your thoughts and feelings, rewrite the script, and th
be willing to receive!

You are the new heroine/hero, and each day you will go out there on the stage
life and live your new role. You will think like the new you, and feel like the n
you. With the help of your anchors, you will do what the new you would c
Realize this: You have been creating every moment of your life so far, witho
knowing it, but now you have the opportunity to take hold of the reins and sta

creating your new script. This is conscious living and this time around you've got an Oscar in your future!

✎ Exercise #33: Rewriting your Script

a. Re-read your life script (exercise #30) and now burn it, yes, I mean literally burn it! Just make sure you have the proper bowl or area so that you don't burn your house down with it.

b. Write out your new script, making any changes that you want for your new life. Make sure to include the new beliefs that will be creating this life.

c. If you need to release some characters, write them each a termination slip, explaining exactly why you are terminating their contract, remembering to surround them in white light, thanking them for the lesson(s) they have taught you (hopefully) and release them to their highest good. (You do not actually need to give your characters their slips in the physical world. They might think you are rather strange, and call the little men and their white coats) You can simply communicate your feelings. If you're not ready to do this in the physical yet, keep working on it in meditation. Often times this will be sufficient.

d. Write out a new contract for any "actors" you would like to cast in this new rewrite of your script, going into full detail about the character traits that you would want them to have.

e. Now film your movie. In other words, make your visualization and include any anchors that you might need. Each time that you run your visualization, create another episode, as if you were watching an ongoing soap opera. The more you play with it, the quicker it will manifest!

Working With Your Inner Child

In all of my years of working with people, I have seen the most profound changes come through work with the inner child. To create a wonderful, new, successful life on paper, all you need to do is create new beliefs, hold the resonance of those new beliefs, and be willing to receive.

However, it is often easier for most people to start by healing the past. Think of it this way: If you carried around a hefty bag all day, filling it with garbage as you went along, then came home in the evening and placed it by your bed, only to get up in the morning and start all over again, how good do you think that bag would smell? Now think of that bag as your life! See what I'm getting at here? Wouldn't you be better off to throw out all the garbage from the day, including the hefty bag, get a new bag and start filling it with flowers? Now you have a pretty sweet smelling life. So let's get started.

For the most part, whoever you are now is simply an extension of who you were then—"then" being your childhood/adolescent years, the years that created most of the beliefs that you still run on today. The strange thing is, we make up our life as we go along, each and every moment. When we look back at our pasts, most of what we think was real was actually made up—by us of course—but nevertheless made up. At times when I have worked with siblings, it was quite amazing to hear two totally different stories about one family! If I hadn't known that they were in the same family I would never have believed it. It's the old story of five different people witnessing a crime and ending up with five different stories of how it occurred.

When you think of a child you of course think of a small adorable person who you love to pick up and hug. But that same adorable little person is also the one who jumps up-and-down stamping her feet, bouncing her arms and screaming, "It's mine, I want it! It's mine," or some such melody. Now, I'm sure that you have seen grown up adults, dressed in their very best Armani suits carrying on with their own version of the childish behavior I've just described. Or almost! And why? Because you or someone else has just pushed one of their buttons.

And what about adolescents? Remember those years? If you've ever been around one for very long, you will know that most of what they think, do and say is totally centered around themselves and their world. I don't know about you but I've met all too many adults who fit this category to a tee!

Now don't get me wrong here, I am not attacking children and adolescents. Actually I prefer working with them than with adults. And the point that's important here is that the behaviors I've been describing are quite normal for us. We act as we do in adolescence because we lacked good models for being conscious adults. It's a little like in the field of medicine, where so much of what they know was derived from studying sick people instead of finding out what makes healthy people healthy. We all need models that draw us toward ways of thinking and being that will help us be healthy and successful.

Think of the circus, you have three arenas, one is for the child, one is for the adolescent and one is for the conscious adult. The show starts, the spotlight floods the arena of the conscious adult, and no one is there to show up. Well, the child, being curious, decides to have a look around. She crawls over to see where the light is coming from. What we have next is a child in the center of the arena where the conscious adult should have been, and she is standing up and taking a bow! Many of us had exactly the same thing happen to us.

Most of us are like that little kid peeking out to the center ring to find out what's going on, only to suddenly discover that the rest of the world is seeing us as an adult. What about your parents, the people who raised you? Maybe you were a little child being raised by a little child. What about your teachers at school? Maybe you were a little child being taught by a little child. What about your lover or spouse? Maybe you are two little children both thinking the other one is the adult!

Would you send a little five-year-old child out into the world to drive your car, do your work, and take care of all your relationships? You might think that's a ridiculous question, but you do it every day. Every time you lose it in your life—get mad, feel guilty, feel not good enough, feel abandoned—whose feelings do you think you're experiencing? Mine? Your next door neighbors? I know that you want to say yours but most of the time these feelings come from that little child or adolescent within you, the ones with all that unfinished business. They're out there, doing your life. It's true!

You're probably wondering how you are going to change all this. Before we get to that, let me explain what is going on here in terms of the bigger picture. You see, because time is simultaneous, your little child/adolescent is alive and doing well or maybe not so well, somewhere out there in time and space. In fact, they will always be out there. Even when you're ninety years old, your child/adolescent will be out there somewhere in the continuum that is time and space. And the thing is, no matter how wonderful a childhood you might have had, you still came from somewhat of a dysfunctional family. There is not a person on the planet who didn't, well maybe one, and even that one, somewhere along the way, felt that someone didn't love them quite enough! That's just the way things are. We were simply never taught to be conscious. Therefore every little child/adolescent is scarred in some way, and what they need is to be nurtured, loved and healed. So now is the time. Heal them!

Let's say a dog bit you when you were five, and for the rest of your life you have been afraid of dogs. If you could go back in time and change the event so that the dog never bit you, you could pretty well say that your fear of dogs would be gone, right? Right! Not only could you say that, but if the fear of dogs was gone, or never existed, then the person you were at five becomes a different person. And you, the adult, are no longer afraid of dogs. By creating that change, small as it might be, you actually created a different life. Without that fear some of the choices and decisions you made along the way would be different, thereby changing your life today. Well, this is how it works. You are going to go back through time, using meditation as your time machine, and change your past, thereby changing your present life. And guess what, this will take you into a brighter future.

The first thing that you need to do is go back into your childhood and think of the things you would change if you could. Because you can! It's never too late to have a happy childhood.

✎ Exercise #34: Healing the Inner Child/Adolescent

a. Sit down and write out all the things from your childhood and adolescence that you would like to change. Start by writing whatever comes to your mind right away. Just let go and write what comes to mind, being careful not to censor yourself in any way.

b. For each of the above, describe exactly how you want to change them. For example, if you were an unwanted child, born into a family already overburdened with problems, you might want to change this picture so that you saw yourself being born into a family where you received quality attention from both parents as well as your siblings.

c. Think of an area in your life where you would like to grow. Then look at the events from your childhood that, if they had been different, would have made it easier for this growth to occur. Imagine these earlier childhood experiences occurring in ways that contribute to this growth. For example, let's say you wanted to grow in the area of self esteem and self-confidence. Quality attention in the scenario in "b," above, would make it easier for you to feel valued and good about yourself. This, in turn, would make it easier for you to grow in the ways that you want.

d. Do the above for your adolescence, in addition to your earlier childhood.

The Healing

Now that you know what you would like to change about your life, this is how you are going to do it. For each person or event that you would have liked to change you will substitute a more positive experience. For instance, let's say your father was emotionally abusive, and you know someone who would be a wonderful father figure. Maybe it's a man from a TV program, such as *Father Knows Best,* which you used to love watching when you were a child. Or if you are from a younger generation, it may have been *Seventh Heaven* that you watched. Maybe it's your best friend's dad, or the man next door. It doesn't matter where you get the father image as long as it is one you can relate to in a totally positive way.

You are simply going to exchange fathers. If the house that you lived in was a shack, and you feel that it caused some of your childhood problems, change it. Create any house that you would have loved to live in. Remember these are meditations. What you create is taking place in your mind so you can create whatever you want—and the thing is, you always do anyway. Now you are creating the experiences to benefit and change your life! The important thing to remember is, if you change it, not only do you change the past but more importantly you change who you are today, which will then allow you to create a brighter future.

If you had a traumatic childhood and the thought of doing a meditation where your tyrannical parent suddenly becomes parent of the year is simply too disconcerting, you can break down the process into baby steps. I absolutely love baby steps, because they can accomplish anything, if you're willing. You might first want to have your higher self act as an intermediary between you and your violent parent. It would look something like this: In your visualization, as your parent (or anyone else) is coming towards you in a violent rage, have your higher self step in to deal with the parent. How do you do that?

You might have your higher self tell the parent that what they are doing is inappropriate behavior and there is no way they will allow that behavior to continue. You might want your higher self to beat them up and lock them in a closet. Or maybe just having your higher self love them would do the trick. You will have a sense for what you need to do.

Feeling like you want to beat up or punish your tyrants for their behavior is natural enough from the child's or adolescent's point of view. However, we know it is inappropriate for adults to still be stuck in those behavior patterns. Remember, whatever happens during meditation is simply meditation. If you feel a need to beat someone up in your imagination, go right ahead. You will not be hauled off to jail! It's better to release those feelings in a meditation than to act them out in your life. And in time the benefits are great. Your inner parents' behavior changes, to be replaced by a nurturing environment that helps your inner child to heal.

The next step might be to have the same intervention with the parent, only this time it is with the child having the self-confidence, and courage—assisted by their higher self, ready to step in to deal with the parent. At some point in the future, you might want to change your parent, so that they become the most wonderful parent on the planet, physically the same but with new behaviors. The choices are always yours!

There are a few ways to work with this process:

1. When I refer to child/adolescent, I am referring to those age periods when the original situation you are going to be healing occurred. In other words, if you were a small child when your mother verbally abused you, you would be working with your child. If the behavior occurred while you were a teenager, then you would be working with your adolescent. It is always good to work with both but take each period separately, not all in one chunk. Remember, baby steps get results.

2. As you work with meditation exercises, memories of your childhood may come rushing back on you. The process is a bit like opening up Pandora's box. Once it's opened you can't go back to the way things were before you started. So don't go running off to hide under the bed. Keep going and the results will be wonderful. As the memories come back, you will simply take those memories into your meditation and change them in ways that will benefit your growth. Example: You remember that on your fifth birthday, your mother dressed you up in a horrendous outfit, and everyone laughed at you. So, when you do your meditation simply go back to the day of your party, have your mother dress you in a great outfit, and watch as everyone comes running up to you telling you how wonderful you look! This technique can transform your past.

3. Use your meditations as your classroom. Think of all the things that you know now, that you would have loved to know then—like all the information in this book! Well, you can accomplish major change in your life by giving all this adult information to your child/adolescent. During

meditation, give the information to your child/adolescent by way of your new, ideal parents or teachers or by you and your higher self. Example: Have the parents of the child/adolescent explain to them that they create their own reality, and when the child/adolescent gets into specific situations let the parents ask them, in a totally supportive way, "Why do you think you created this situation, and what is your lesson?"

4. While you are going through these changes in your life, you may encounter feelings that you think a sane person would never ask for. Example: Sharon created a job that she had wanted for years in Los Angeles. She was all packed and ready to go when she started to question her move. Understanding how the inner child worked, she immediately went into meditation. When she arrived her inner child was crying, explaining that she was afraid to move, because she might not have any friends to play with. Sharon immediately told her child, that their new next-door neighbor in Los Angeles was a little girl who was waiting for little Sharon to come and be her best friend and that she had a brand-new Teddy bear to give to her when little Sharon arrived. At that moment little Sharon's face lit up and she stated that she was ready to move. Needless to say Sharon came out of meditation and went about the business of getting packed.

Please note in Sharon's example that it was not her, the conscious adult who was feeling resistant about going to Los Angeles. It was her child/adolescent. In most cases where you are feeling resistant to a positive change that you have consciously chosen to make in your life, your resistance will be coming from your child/adolescent. So go right into a quick meditation and ask that inner child/adolescent what they're feeling. Your mission in the meditation is to hear their feelings and then give them or tell them whatever will make them happy. Bribery—such as a new Teddy bear, works wonders. Remember, it's just a meditation. Once your child/adolescent is happy, you can leave the meditation knowing that the issue is handled. You will open your eyes and feel wonderful.

Working with your inner child/adolescent might take awhile. Not all changes will happen overnight, though you may be surprised at how many do. However, I believe that these techniques for creating a happy childhood are some of the most important things you can do to further your growth, create success and allow you to awaken to the person you really are. Even after you get the sense that your inner child and adolescent are healed, it's a good idea to go back and visit with them every month or so. Remember, they will always exist out there someplace, in time and space. So simply go into meditation and hang out with them. Spend a whole day (according to a meditation clock) doing whatever they like to do, and it will only take a few minutes of your time. Nurturing your inner child/adolescent will help to keep your life in balance.

✎ Exercise #35: Changing Your Inner History

In the following meditation, you will be changing the images, thoughts, and feelings of your childhood and adolescence and bringing them alive in your inner world.

Inner Child/Adolescent Meditation

Find a quiet place where there will be no interruptions for at least fifteen minutes. Take a few moments to relax, then close your eyes and get into a meditation where you feel relaxed in your body and mind. Imagine that you are in a safe and beautiful place in nature, where your higher self waits for you. Tell your higher self that you are now willing and ready to allow the complete healing of your inner child and adolescent. (Choose one or the other to work on at a time.) Ask your higher self to help you with this healing.

After you have arrived at your beautiful place in nature, notice a bridge across a river or other division of land. On the other side of the bridge, a child waits for you. As you gaze across the way, you see that this child is you, at whatever age you are now looking at her or him.

Now imagine walking toward the bridge and then crossing it. Just as you reach the other side, your little child leaps into your arms and you embrace her or him. You introduce yourself, explaining that you and her/him are the same person. You have come to the child from his/her future in order to help them in their present life. You then introduce the child to their higher self, which is, of course, your own higher self.

Having completed the introductions, and the "reunion," the three of you head for home. Home is the house where you lived as a child. If you have difficult or painful memories associated with that house, you can have any house that you wish. That may be the one where you now live or a place that pleases you in every way.

Once home, you put the child to sleep. You remain at a distance, watchful as the new day begins. As the new day starts, you create all the experiences you need to give your inner child everything they need to grow up in a way that will fully support the growth you wish to have in your adult life at this time.

You do not need to complete the entire past for your child right now. But understand that you can come back to this place any time you wish, and you can keep running the "movie" in your mind, return a few times every week, just as you might watch a serial movie or a soap opera as the new story your are creating unfolds. Each time you come back to your inner child, you will be changing his or her experiences so that they fully support the goals you have chosen in your adult life.

You would ideally carry this exercise for recreating your past through both your childhood and adolescence.

Understanding Fear

I don't have to tell you that when fear comes into your life, it can twist your arms, your neck, and your heart. Then it will hang you up by your toenails and make you do all kinds of things, none of which you would probably enjoy…and most of it will never help you in any way, shape or form to create value in your life. But having said that, there are those times—doing the material in this book, for instance—where your handling short periods of fear will lead to an awakening and a liberation to have the quality of life you long to have. While fear might be an initial reaction, you will move forward to hear what your higher self has been trying to get you to understand.

It's important to know that your higher self has always been with you but your old fears and old programming told you not to listen. You were unwilling to listen to the whispers and possibly even the screams. Your higher self has no other option, but to make use of the terror that sometimes comes when the nightmare of your unconsciousness lets go and you awaken to your truth. In this case your fear can be the catalyst of positive change.

It's funny how we think that only people like us have fear, and that successful people don't. Well, I'm here to tell you that successful people have just as many fears as you have. Maybe even more. But they don't let their fears immobilize them, like the other ninety percent of the population. They take their fear and just do it anyway. If you ever toured any locker rooms before a big game, or visited the dressing rooms of famous stars, you would hear the toilets flushing, believe me! Some of those people are so nervous that they're vomiting, having diarrhea, and peeing in their pants. But does that stop them? Absolutely not! They go out there and do what they have to do. That's why they're successful, they can be who they are in spite of their fear.

A friend of mine who coaches best selling authors and lecturers told me that if he wasn't bound to secrecy he could give me a long list of famous writers who totally freak out before doing presentations. He said, "Why do you think they have bathrooms in the dressing rooms on shows like *Oprah Winfrey* and *Good Morning, America?*" Next time your favorite star doesn't come out on stage exactly on cue, you'll know why.

Spiritual teachers tell us there are only two emotions in the universe— love and fear. If you're not coming from love, then you're coming from fear. Earth is a fear-based planet. So when you start out on this path to consciousness you might feel a little like a salmon swimming against the current. It can seem like you are the only one going in the direction you are, and really wonder if you are doing the right thing. You can be literally bombarded by fear from all around you, from the newspapers you read, the television you watch, and most of the people in your life. The good news is that the world is changing, with more and more people awakening, and each one gives support to the others.

We are definitely living in an age of awakening. There are dozens of books written on handling our fear, so clearly it's an important subject. Without knowing how to handle our fear we are literally trapped in our little mud puddles of mediocrity. Now, here's the thing that I want you to know about fear, then you can go out and read all the books you want: Fear is an illusion. It is not real! Let's do it again: Fear is an illusion. It is not real! It is false evidence appearing real. You are allowing yourself to be lead around by the nose, by something that is not even real! Write that on the billboards. Place it on your refrigerator, or better yet your television. Get it tattooed on your forehead, but get it!

Listen, it's okay if you feel like a fool, now that you know that you realize that your illusions have been leading you around like a trained organ grinder's monkey! Maybe that's just what you needed to step out of the illusion.

Is fear ever healthy? Sure it is. Think of walking down a dark alley at three o'clock in the morning and suddenly hearing footsteps behind you. Now, that is healthy fear. It could save your life by alerting you to get the heck out of there.

Most of the fear we struggle with in our daily lives, however, is related either to the past or to the future but not the present. Think about that. Your fears about being successful, about having the life you long for are rooted either in something that once happened, causing you to be afraid it might happen again, or it is a fear that something just possibly could happen at some point in the future. Once again, these are illusions. They are very different than being faced by a truck bearing down on you at seventy miles an hour or a gang of hoodlums following you in a dark alley.

The question is, "What do I do about these illusions of fear that I have? They sure feel real when I'm in the middle of them." And I will give you the answer in the form of a question. And the question is…what is the opposite of fear? That's your answer! Love. Love is the answer, always was, and always will be. And in this case, love in the form of faith.

God/Goddess is the highest frequency of love and in loving and believing in God/Goddess you have faith. Faith is the knowing that something exists even when you don't have the tangible evidence to prove it. If you only knew who walks beside you, you would never feel fear again. And here's the crux of the problem—that most of us do not have an intimate relationship with God/Goddess. We do not know that we have these incredible unseen spirit friends who are here to support, guide and protect us. And how do you get to this place of faith? Well, I'm not going to lie to you, you have to work at it. It's not something you can go out and buy or just be given, unless it was already given to you as a belief from childhood. And just knowing this information as raw knowledge will not do the trick either. You need to own it as part of your wisdom and live it daily! In a world such as ours, where so many of us were programmed not to believe in such things, it is a question of learning or remembering who we really are. Once you do that, you will make the transition from fear to a place of knowing and love so much easier.

Isn't it strange to think that the one thing—faith—which would make our lives so much easier, not to mention more fulfilled, we have pushed away from us, leaving us nearly defenseless in our own ignorance. Because we have made ourselves so grandiose and arrogant, the thought of believing in God/Goddess, and having the faith to back that belief up, has become something that we do only in private, if we do it at all—in the closet, so to speak. And even then, it's not an actual intimate relationship for most people; it is simply an act by rote. People don't actually speak about God/Goddess. Because if they did, they would be seen as those religious fanatics that people make jokes about.

This is what we have come to! Of course we do have the one day that we allow ourselves to go and believe in God/Goddess outwardly. However, that's mostly for social purposes anyway! And now, after all that programming, learning to live this thing called faith is sometimes like trying to believe in Santa Claus or the Tooth Fairy again. Oh to be one of those people who was given the gift of faith from the beginning! Well, that sounds to me like we need to go back to our inner child and teach them very well.

But don't despair! I have given you exercises to help you through your bouts with fear and to better identify where your fear is coming from. Even so, it is ultimately faith that will dissolve your fears.

Sometimes our fears are so remote and elusive that we almost can't even fathom them. For instance, before I was born my parents had a little girl who died when she was four days old. From the moment I was conceived my mother was enveloped in the fear that they would lose me, too. It was as if I was bathed in her fears and my father's fears even when I was growing in my mother's womb. So I know what it's like to deal with fear of the most baffling kind. And I can tell you that it's not always easy. However, when you have this knowledge, work with it and you will eventually surrender your fear to God/Goddess, who then allows you to deal with your fear at a manageable level. You, too, will be able to just take it and go where you need to go—straight to success, fulfillment, joy and love and, of course, fun!

✎ Exercise #36: Understanding Fear

a. Make a list of the main things you fear. For example, maybe you fear being abandoned and alone, or you are afraid of falling into poverty. Simply write these down in the simplest way that you can.

b. For any area of your life where you are working to grow and change, describe the fears that you feel are preventing you from accomplishing what you want. For example, maybe you would like to have more self-confidence. But you find that every time you think of acting more confidently there is a fearful little voice inside you that cries out, "Who do you think you are? You are going to just fall on your face!"

c. Create baby steps to accomplish the changes you want, recognizing that you must change your fears as you go along. For instance, don't think of "becoming more self-confident" as a single big step but as many smaller ones. One way to do this is to look at an area in your life where your fears come up for you but not in a very serious way. One person found that her fear and lack of self-confidence came up every time her friends at work asked here which restaurant she would like to go out to for lunch. This happened every Friday, and she always left the choice up to other people because it brought up too much fear for her. However, this turned out to be the first of many small baby steps she made toward becoming more self-confident and learning to trust the choices she made.

Carefully make up a list of these baby steps, going from the easiest and simplest to the most difficult and complex. Then set some goals, including notes about when and how you will achieve each step in the weeks or months ahead.

Then, set out and start walking that path of baby steps, moving ever-closer to your goals for growth and change that will make your life better.

e. Write a letter to yourself, giving you permission to let go of your fear to be free to be the successful person you have chosen to be. Also forgive yourself for choosing to be anything less.

f. Celebrate each baby step as you accomplish it. You can do this by simply checking it off your list or lighting a candle (the simplest ritual) or by rewarding yourself with a special treat.

g. Here's a fun thing to do: Get into your most adventurous and creative child mode and do a drawing of your fear. Then pin the drawing on the wall where you can see it clearly, choose some music that seems to express your fear, and dance that fear, really get into it, letting it release from your body through your movements. When you are done, burn the drawing, really burn it, finally dispelling the fear in smoke (be sure to burn it in a safe place such as a fireplace or backyard barbecue.)

h. Close your eyes. Think of your fear and imagine it being contained inside a balloon. Imagine this fear growing, getting larger and larger, expanding the balloon until it is so huge that it bursts. Then visualize the feeling of inner peace and confidence (or other feelings) that you are wanting to create.

Or, think about your fear as a large, dark circle or disk or cloud in front of you. It can be as large as you want when you start. Then imagine it growing smaller and smaller, and going out of focus. Mentally push it away as far as you can, knowing you have the power to do this. Finally, shove it way out into space, somewhere behind the sun.

j. Pray. Surrender your fear. Thank God/Goddess for taking it and for co-creating an alternative with you, embracing and affirming your highest good.

k. Practice these processes frequently. Get into the habit of doing one or more of them any time you feel fear attached to anything you have to do immediately. Do the process that works best for you, but do it before your fear can expand and prevent you from taking action.

A Helpful Meditation for Conquering Fear

Close your eyes and go into a meditation where you feel your body and mind deeply relax. Imagine yourself at your beautiful place in nature, where your higher self waits for you. As you greet your higher self, tell her or him that you are now willing and ready to surrender your fear and ask for their help. They will then take you by the hand and bring you to a very beautiful place where you open to all your senses, fully allowing in all the beauty around you.

You higher self then gives you a magic potion to drink. They touch you in a way that will transform the energy of your body. Almost instantly, you realize that you are wearing a costume, that your old fears and self-denial are contained in this costume that you had thought was your body. You unzip this costume, just as you might unzip a jump suit that you have been wearing. You simply step out of it, allowing the old costume to drop to the ground in a heap.

Watch as this body suit falls to the ground. Inside it, you will see what looks like any old decaying root. It is the root of your fears, withering away to nothing, even as you watch, then fizzles into a flame that turns the whole thing to ash that blows away in the wind.

You now look into a beautiful deep pool of water by a spring, where your higher self has brought you, and as you look in you see that you are a beautiful light being.

For a moment, as you and your higher self stand beside this beautiful pond in this wonderful place in nature, the two of you talk about how your life is going to be, freed of your fears forever. Together you paint brilliant mind pictures of the life ahead of you. Then, both of you fly joyfully away together.

You now come out of your meditation, knowing that you have brought this process to completion. It's done and it is time to go forward with actions that are supported by all that you have done to make these changes in your life.

Learning to Receive

Every one of us has a list of those things we've always wanted and have never gotten. We see our friends, our next-door neighbors, our relatives, and even those people we like the least, having what we want. We may even find ourselves wondering, "What's wrong with me? What am I doing wrong?" And the answer is, you're not doing anything wrong. You already have what you want!

"Now hold on for a moment," you're probably saying. You're wondering where it is. Is she crazy? I don't see what she's talking about here. And I'll have to agree with you. You don't see it because it's behind a door, a door you have been unwilling to open. Everything you have ever wanted—assuming that it's for your highest good—is right there behind that door.

I'll bet I can guess what you are about to say now: "Key please!"

The key is your willingness to receive, which for the most part you have been unwilling to use. I know that sounds a bit weird. However, once again you have been programmed by a world that tells you life is a struggle, you can't have everything you want, stop reaching for the stars, etc. I'm sure these statements sound familiar to you. And no wonder! They have become consensus reality, shared by us all. They've been programmed right into your computer, becoming part of your belief systems almost without your noticing it. And you know by now, once it's in there it is there to stay—unless you choose to change it.

Speaking of the word choose, let me tell you that it is better to use the word "choose" instead of the word "want." When you want something, you remain in a state of wanting, of not having what you desire. However, the word choose implies that you are choosing that which you desire. The difference is subtle but important.

Getting back to the key for receiving: I want you to start thinking of receiving as simply an energy. It will go to anyone who allows it into their life. It is not a question of who deserves, since everyone deserves. We are all God's/Goddess' children, or a part of God/Goddess, whichever way you like to think of it. Who receives is only a question of who is willing to receive.

So how do we become willing? Well, if you have come this far in the book and if you've done all your homework, you know, eaten all your broccoli, then these cookies are closer then you realize. If you haven't done the work, sorry kids, but no cookies. That's how it works! But how could I ever doubt you? I'm sure you've all done your work, so I'm going to give you the answers. Start by thinking about why you desire whatever you do and don't give any attention to how. How is your higher self's job, and together with God/Goddess you will co-create it. Make sure you are going in the right direction. Sounds funny, huh? Well, like the bible story of Lot's wife who turned to salt when she looked back, we all seem to face backwards in our life—towards the past! We think of all the things that either went wrong or that never went at all and we get stuck thinking and feeling, "What's the point? It will only turn out like that again. It always goes that way." At that point we stay seated in our little mud puddle of discomfort and do nothing. Or maybe these self-defeating beliefs are hidden in your subconscious. In that case, we may act but only to create the same frustrating result again because the negative belief is back there, shooting down all our best efforts. (Those who have done their homework already know this, of course.)

Think of each moment as a brand new, beautiful clump of potentiality waiting for you to create something magnificent. Just remember to face in the right direction, which is towards the future not the past. Then go forward and just DO IT!

When my daughter was growing up, I used to tell her that life was better then having a gold Bloomingdales' credit card, because everything is already given to you. Well, before you start dashing off to Bloomingdales', demanding everything you choose, you need to do a little work.

✎ Exercise #37: Learning to Receive

Even after you have cleared away whatever was standing in the way of achieving the life you want, and after you have created a clear mental image of your future life, there is one more step to take. That step has to do with opening yourself up to receive. Unless you are able to receive what the universe offers you will simply not let it in. The receiving exercise has three parts: 1) Giving Yourself Permission; 2) The Dance of Receiving; and 3) the Meditation:

Giving Yourself Permission

In this exercise, you are training your consciousness that action follows any thoughts and intentions that you express. It's a simple exercise to do. Every time you do some everyday task, such as opening a door, or picking up your fork, or getting into the shower in the morning, stop for a moment. Then give yourself permission to do what you are about to do anyway: "I now give myself permission to open this door." Then go ahead and open the door or do whatever else it is you were intending to do.

Once you have done this a while, your mind gets the idea that each time you give yourself permission to do something, you actually go ahead and do it. Our unconscious minds will assume that when you give yourself permission to do anything—whether it is opening a door or starting a successful business or creating a loving relationship, you naturally go ahead and do just that.

All you have to do is carry out this exercise two or three times a day, in the morning and in the evening, and you will have developed the inner patterns that expect success any time you give yourself permission.

Dance of Receiving

Ask your higher self to be with you and explain that you are ready and willing to receive. Find some beautiful music that you feel portrays the experience of receiving. Dance to this music, putting all your feelings of what you would like to be receiving into your body, allowing those feelings to create your dance. With outstretched arms, invite to you all that you are to receive.

Meditation to Receive

As with the other meditations that you have been learning in this book, find your beautiful place in nature and make yourself comfortably at home in this place. Close your eyes and create a wonderful mental picture of the energy of receiving. It might appear to you as a brilliant white light. It might take a human form or you might see it as a rich landscape bathed in crystal-bright sunlight. Whatever the image happens to be for you, let it come in. Then sit and make contact with it. If it is a human form you might speak with it. If it is light you might dance with it, basking in its warm rays. Whatever this energy happens to be, whatever form it takes, be sure to interact with it, so that you feel totally comfortable and at one with it, giving yourself full and total permission to let it become part of your life.

Anchoring Your Wish List

Write down all the things you want to create in your life. Then take each item on the list and think about how it would feel to already have it in your life. When you really get a strong sense of how this will feel, create an anchor. With your anchor in place, create the image of what you want as if it were sitting in the space right in front of you, close enough to reach out and touch. Make the image larger, clearer, and bring it in as close to you as you possibly can, with all the feelings associated with totally receiving whatever it is, still comfortable and fulfilling for you.

Do this two to three times a day, and voila, it will be yours!

The Fine Art of Forgiveness

I'm sure you've all heard those famous last words, "I'll forgive, but I won't forget."

What is it about forgiveness that makes it so difficult for us to do? The answer is that we are usually into our child or adolescent hurt. This is truly the source of so many of our problems! As conscious adults most of us realize that forgiveness is not for the benefit of the person we are forgiving. Rather it is for our own benefit. By forgiving we release ourselves from the toxic emotions of anger, fear, resentment, and—worst case scenario—REVENGE! We know that if we don't let it go, if we hold onto the grievance rather than forgiving, these toxic feelings will fester and grow, creating blockages or even disease in, guess who? You and me, the people who are stubbornly refusing to forgive. Moreover, when we hold onto our grievances, this toxic stuff, we close the door to receiving. We are telling God/Goddess, "No, I am not ready to receive the good that is coming to me." We are just spinning our wheels, going nowhere but burning up a lot of energy!

If you have been following the previous lessons carefully—and I am sure you have—you would know that you are the one who created the situation. Remember? You and your friend made a deal your last time around to play out exactly the script that is causing you so much trouble right now. You brought in this person who you now need to forgive.

Now, you might be scratching your head wondering why you brought them in. Don't you remember? No, you should not remember because you've got celestial amnesia about the deal you made, right? At least I hope that's the case because if it isn't all this grief you are going through won't pay off. Clearly this is a difficult lesson. Nevertheless, doesn't it seem odd that you would go through this whole process of bringing in one of your dear friends from home, asking them to help you with this lesson, and then, after they have done such a good job for you, you got caught up in your anger and hurt, wondering whether you should forgive her or not.

I knew when you looked at this logically you would understand! See how simple life really is? The key is always to realize that no one else is controlling you, that no one else can make you do, be, or feel any specific way. It is all your show, your production and the sooner you take hold of the reins and become empowered by the truth, the sooner you will start to experience the real joy of your life.

✎ Exercise #38: Forgiveness

It has often been said that the most difficult people in our lives are often our greatest teachers. Often, we have to go through the process of forgiveness before we can get the lessons they have brought into our lives. That's what this exercise is designed to do, to strip away the veils that hide these valuable lessons.

Step 1: Make a List

Make a list of the people who you feel grievances about. This may involve recalling relationships from the past.

Step 2: Take Responsibility

Assume it is true that before you came into this life you made a pact with these people to play out the scripts that you have with each other, just as we have discussed in the pages of this book. To the best of your ability, look at each of the people on your list and explain why you created the relationship you did with them. What was it that you wanted them to teach you.

Step 3: Forgiveness Meditation

Close your eyes, go into a meditation, relax your body and mind, then find your way to your safe and beautiful place in nature. Greet your higher self who is there waiting for you.

Let your higher self know that you are totally ready and willing to forgive. When you are ready, bring the people that you are willing to forgive at this moment and place them in front of you. (You may choose to do one at a time or have them appear as a group.)

Choosing one person at a time, tell them how you feel. Explain why you were angry or hurt, then go on to say that you now realize they have only done what you and they had agreed upon prior to the time that you came into this life. Tell them that you are now ready to give up this pain or anger and forgive them so that you can both get the lessons involved and move on.

Feel the anger, hurt or resentment and bring these into your solar plexus (stomach area). As you do this, visualize these feelings as a red light. Visualize a opening in your solar plexus and imagine all the red light escaping, blending with the light beyond it, which is pure white.

Now fill your heart area with the warm, pink light of gratitude and love. Visualize an opening in your heart, allowing the pink light to surround the person you are forgiving as you tell them that both of you are now released to more fully realize the lessons you were brought here to teach each other, and that these lessons are now available to us for the highest good. ~

GETTING READY FOR COMPLETION

Here's another one of those famous sayings: "All things come to an end." But then, someone always tacks onto that, "And then they begin again."

You will get to a certain point in your spiritual work when you will experience a feeling of completion. You have done your job and now the time has come for you to let go, release it all into the hands of God/Goddess, *knowing* that it will be done. It is here, with the word "knowing," that the difficulty starts for most of us. Because many of your dreams might not have turned out exactly as you wanted, it is very easy to lose faith. Even easier to lose *knowingness*. Think of a farmer who has just planted his crop of potatoes. He doesn't go out to the field everyday digging up the ground to see where his potatoes are, wondering if and when they will come in. He has the faith to know that they will be there at the appropriate time.

So, when you have completed this book and done the exercises, you've got your potatoes planted. You have created a new path for yourself, one that will lead to new opportunities for growth, love, abundance, fun, and joy! Just put your arms out and let the universe know that you're willing to receive. Surrender to God/Goddess. Love and be patient with yourself. Realize that we are all one and we all have love for this sacred one.

Choose to do something each day that will bring love into another person's life. It'll make them and the Angels smile. And when you come home, feel love coming around to you from every direction.

And now, I thank you for holding this book in your hands and touching my heart, for you have allowed me to be the vehicle through which God/Goddess has touched your heart!

All My Love,
Barbra

ABOUT THE AUTHOR

Barbra Gilman has twenty years experience as a therapist. Her workshop, *Living Life Eyes Wide Open,* became the focus of her attention after realizing that most people were seeking answers that could not be found in therapy alone. Her workshop was the inspiration and basis for this book. She is an Interfaith Minister and CEO of Success Strategies For Life, a firm assisting families, couples, companies and individuals in developing their full potential. Barbra served as the Director of the Center for Spiritual Awareness in New York and has hosted her own radio show, "Conscious Choices." She is a popular lecturer and has taught hundreds of workshops on personal and spiritual development and success through awareness. She is a Certified Parent Educator with the International Network for Children and Families teaching "Redirecting Children's Behavior" courses, which offer parents, teachers, and other adults who care about the welfare of our "new children," insights and behaviors to empower them to develop our young people's inherent abilities so that they can complete their roles as "peace makers" in the world. Barbra trains those interested in becoming RCB trainers across the country. She is a contributing author to *The Indigo Children: Book II.*

To contact Barbra for lectures, tapes, workshops or private consultations:
Email: *Barbraspks@aol.com*
Website: *www.BarbraGilman.com*
Phone: 888-826-8930

ANNOTATED BIBLIOGRAPHY

The Abraham Material (audio tapes) is wonderful for beginners as well as for those who have been on the path for awhile. This information on reality creation is not only simple to learn but life changing when lived. You'll discover that you are free to choose that new avenues for joy will open up to you. One of the most valuable lessons for me in this material was that in our joy we grow, and in our joyous growth we add to the growth experience of All-That-Is. Available through the website: www.Abraham-Hicks.com, or call 830-755-2299.

The *Conversations with God* trilogy (published by Hampton Roads Publishing). These are my all-time favorite books. Neil Donald Walsh has us gazing into the cosmological mysteries at the heart of our universe, asking new questions about life and finding a new vision and new understanding of our relationship to the universe. The author clears away a new path for us to reclaim our spiritual connection with each other and to experience a more intimate and loving connection with God.

The Nature of Personal Reality—a Seth Book, by Jane Roberts (published by Prentice Hall). This was my introduction to the concept of creating our own reality. This book changed my life for evermore. This will always be a classic in reality creation.

The Lazaris Material. (audio tapes) For someone who has gotten the first stages of reality creation under their belts I highly recommend this material. The audio tapes are seminars in themselves, with techniques and meditations pointing out potential pitfalls and distractions that could otherwise obscure our vision and detain us from reaching our destination. Lazaris offers suggestions that can allow magic, and miracles. This work is for serious students who are willing to put time and effort into their growth. Lazaris has said: "Turn up your light. For, even if you do not know where you are going, it will be brighter when you get there." Available through the website: www.Lazaris.com or by calling 800-678-2356.

The Kryon Material. For a more cosmological perspective there is the *Kryon* material which speaks of the source and explores the attributes of basic cosmic energy. It is a total crossover of mainstream science and the New Age. If you like physics, you will like this. If you like astronomy, you will like this. If you like how the love of God plays into it all…you will like this! Available through the website: www.Kryon.com or by calling 800-352-6657.

Spirit Circle by Hal Zina Bennett. (Tenacity Press) This is a magical story of universal mysteries and ancient shamanic spiritual traditions that pulls the reader into its spell! Though a novel, it is based on a series of visions and channelings by the author and includes a dramatic prophecy that describes our spiritual roles in the unfolding millenium. A great find when you are looking for a way to introduce someone new to this journey. At most bookstores or call the publisher at 800-738-6721.

Printed in the United States
80812LV00004B/67